Performance
READING

Continental Press
Elizabethtown, PA 17022

Program Advisors

Charline Barnes, Department of Curriculum and Instruction, University of Northern Iowa, Cedar Falls, Iowa.
Andrew Biemiller, Institute of Child Study, University of Toronto, Toronto, Canada.
Wood Smethurst and **Martha Burdette,** Ben Franklin Academy, Atlanta, Georgia.

Project Director: Beth Spencer
Project Editor: Megan Bergonzi
Design and Composition: David Stirba, Catherine Magaro
Art Direction: Crystal L. Crater
Illustrations: Diane Appelt, David Stirba

Photo Credits

Photo Courtesy of New Mexico/Energy, Minerals and Natural Resources Department/Forestry Division/Smokey Bear Historical Park: Page 6
© **AFP/Corbis:** Page 8; Page 62; Cover, Page 1, Page 69, *Sammy Sosa*
© **Raymond Gehman/Corbis:** Page 9, *lookout tower;* Page 20, *all photos;* Page 21
© **Penny Tweedie/Corbis:** Page 10, *tent city*
© **Gary Braasch/Corbis:** Page 15
© **Digital Vision:** Page 7, Page 16, *lava*
© **Tony Arruza/Corbis:** Page 7, Page 19, *Hurricane Andrew*
© **Roger Ressmyer/Corbis:** Page 23; Page 26, *celebration*
© **Patrick Bennett/Corbis:** Page 25, *bus*
© **Own Franken/Corbis:** Page 26, *polls*
© **Jacques M. Chenet/Corbis:** Page 27
© **Bettmann/Corbis:** Page 28, *Truman;* Page 29
© **Reuters NewMedia Inc./Corbis:** Page 28, *Bush*
© **Annie Griffiths Belt/Corbis:** Page 50
© **Don Dickson:** Page 55, *Mars ERV*
© **Robert Murray Pioneer Astronautics:** Page 56, *people on Mars*
© **John Frassanito and Associates/NASA:** Page 56, *Ground Rover*
© **Duomo/Corbis:** Page 61, *Sammy Sosa;* Page 67
© **Stephen Green:** Page 69, *Wrigley Field*
© **Cydney Conger/Corbis:** Page 72; Page 75
© **Craig Aurness/Corbis:** Page 74, *house*
© **Robert Rogers/Tampa Bay Devil Rays:** Page 80, *all photos;* 81, *Jim Morris*
Photos Courtesy of Toyota Motor Sales, U. S. A., Inc.: Page 25, *Prius and SUV*
Photos provided by Keystone-Mast Collection, UCR/California Museum of Photography, University of California at Riverside: Page 45, *all photos*
Photo Courtesy of Smart Home, Inc.: Page 74, *remote*
Corbis Images, Inc.: Cover, Page 1, *helicopter;* Cover, Page 1, Page 52, *covered wagon;* Cover, Page 1, Page 56, *astronaut in space suit;* Page 7, Page 10, *firemen walking from fire;* Page 10, *firemen fighting fire;* Page 25, *construction worker;* Page 32, *compact disc;* Page 33; Page 36; Page 51; Page 52; Page 74, *kitchen*
PhotoDisc, Inc.: Page 9; Page 10, *smokejumper;* Page 11; Page 14; Page 32, *snowplow;* Page 38, *all photos;* Page 41; Page 46; Page 54; Page 55, *Mars;* Page 61, *naturalization ceremony;* Page 63; Page 64, *all;* Page 65; Page 70; Page 73, *Amish children;* Page 74, *Amish buggy;* Page 77; Page 81, *bat and ball*
EyeWire, Inc.: Page 44; Page 47; Page 57; Page 60; Page 61, *remote;* Page 73, *keypad*

ISBN 0-8454-9360-4
© 2002 The Continental Press, Inc.

Continental Press
Elizabethtown, PA 17022

CONTENTS

Pretest

Choose the best word to finish each sentence.

competition	escape	popular	opportunities
available	valuable	security	automatically
direction	exchanged	protect	distributed

1. There are three apartments _____ for rent in our building.

2. The coach _____ permission slips for the field trip on Thursday.

3. We are going to a gymnastics _____ in New Jersey this weekend.

4. The dog was able to _____ from the flooded house.

5. The mother bear stayed nearby to _____ her cubs.

6. The workmen lost many _____ tools in the accident.

7. Luis and I _____ telephone numbers.

8. The door to the grocery store opened _____ when I stood in front of it.

9. The alarm to our neighbor's _____ system went off last night.

10. Hamburgers are the most _____ item on the menu.

11. The crab crawled in the _____ of the ocean.

12. You will have many _____ to succeed in life if you stay in school.

Write the root word for each of these words.

distributed _____   direction _____

automatically _____   competition _____

Was Smokey a Real Bear?

You may have seen Smokey Bear on television commercials. He always asks people to prevent forest fires. But did you know that there was a real Smokey Bear?

In the 1950s a bear cub was found in a forest in New Mexico surrounded by flames. To escape the forest fire, the cub had climbed up a tree. Some firefighters found the scared and hungry cub hanging onto a burned tree trunk. The firefighters were so moved by the brave little cub that they named him Smokey and took him to an animal doctor. When Smokey was well, he was sent to live at the National Zoo in Washington, D.C. Millions of people visited him every year.

Although this bear cub grew old and eventually passed away, the message that "Only you can prevent forest fires" is carried on with the spirit of Smokey Bear.

Smokey Bear asks people to help prevent forest fires.

1. Which of these tells the main idea of the passage? Underline the best answer.
   A Smokey Bear is on television commercials.
   B A real bear cub came to be a symbol against forest fires.
   C Smokey Bear was found on a burned tree trunk.
   D Millions of people visited the cub at the National Zoo.

2. Which word in the passage means "to keep from happening"?

   _____

3. Why do you think the firefighters named the cub and sent him to live in the National Zoo?

   _____

   _____

4. Explain what Smokey's message that "Only you can prevent forest fires" means in your own words.

   _____

   _____

Fire and water are necessary for living, but we can't always control them. When they get out of control, they cause real trouble.

- Wildfires and forest fires can be caused by lightning or by people. It takes firefighters with special skills and courage to battle these dangerous fires.

- Volcanoes don't blow very often, but when they do, there's big trouble. In 1980, Mount St. Helens blew lava and rocks for a full day. How can a volcano be controlled?

- Hurricane Andrew reached speeds of 165 miles and hour as it blew across Florida in 1992. People came from all over the United States to help Andrew's victims get their lives back together.

Lightning Strikes!

All summer the weather in Idaho had been hot and dry. The signs near the National Forest said, "Fire Danger: Extreme." Everyone knew what this meant. Be extra careful with matches. Don't leave campfires unattended. But no one can prevent lightning from striking, and sure enough, that is what happened one night.

The lightning struck a tall tree far from the road. The tree was so dry that it burst into flames. It was a windy night, and the fire spread rapidly. By morning, park employees were going from house to house in nearby towns. They told people to vacate the area. The fire would soon reach their homes.

extreme	*adj.* great, strong
unattended	*adj.* not watched or cared for
prevent	*v.* stop something before it happens
rapidly	*adv.* quickly
employees	*n.* workers
vacate	*v.* leave

Read each of these sentences. Then choose one word from above to fill in each blank.

1. When the carton fell on the floor, the milk poured out _____.

2. Pets should not be left _____ in cars.

3. Always wear sunscreen to _____ sunburn.

4. The boss asked the _____ to arrive early for work.

5. We had to _____ the building during the fire drill.

6. We wore heavy coats, hats, and gloves in the _____ cold.

Fire!

To a firefighter, summertime is "fire season." Each year in the United States, there can be as many as 100,000 wildfires. Sometimes hundreds of fires are burning at the same time. These grass and forest fires are mostly in the western states, but they can pop up anywhere. When there are large fires, firefighters come from across the country to try to prevent them from spreading. They travel from fire to fire. Their job is hot, difficult, and dangerous. They have to work together, and they rely on many other workers to help them.

Summertime is wildfire season in the United States.

How Do Fires Start?

As long as there have been forests, there have been forest fires. Before people lived near forests, lightning started most fires. Nobody was there to put these fires out. In fact, many people are surprised to learn that fires can be *good* for forests. Fires can clean out the **debris** that has built up on the ground. These old, dry leaves and branches that have fallen make fires more dangerous. Certain kinds of pine trees need the heat of a fire for their pine cones to release their seeds. Even some forest animals need fires. They run away during the fire, then eat the plants that begin to grow soon after the fire is out.

> **debris:** *n. scattered remains of something broken*
>
> After the storm, the road was covered with **debris.**

Now, most forest fires are started by people. Sometimes all it takes is one spark from an unattended campfire. Some fires burn out by themselves. They burn the forest floor, but they do not travel to the crowns, or tops, of the trees. But when the weather is extremely dry and windy, a fire can spread rapidly. Then it can reach nearby homes. These are the fires that must be stopped.

Before firefighters can fight a fire, first they must find it.

Fighting the Fire

In many national forests, there are towers called "lookout towers." Employees called "rangers" work in the towers. They watch for smoke that tells them a fire has started. Sometimes airplanes are used to spot smoke. They have special equipment to "sense" a fire. If a fire is moving quickly or is near places where people live, rangers try to prevent the fire from spreading. They might also tell people to vacate the area.

All fires need three things: heat, fuel, and oxygen. To fight a fire, one of these three things must be taken away. The fuel in a forest fire is anything that can burn, such as dead branches or dry leaves. Firefighters often cut a "fire line" to block the fire from its fuel. A fire line is a strip of land where all the trees and brush have been removed. To remove the oxygen from a fire, firefighters spray water or dump chemicals on it.

Working Together

Smokejumpers are men and women from all walks of life. Some are teachers, students, and graduates of the forestry and agricultural fields. They all bring unique experiences to help fight forest fires.

When fires start deep in the forest where there are no roads, special firefighters who are called "smokejumpers" use parachutes to get to the fire. Smokejumpers must carry packs that weigh over 100 pounds. Teams of these firefighters jump into the fire area from planes. The planes then drop boxes with their equipment and food nearby.

Many people are needed to fight fires. Some are in charge of planning. Other people work in the first-aid tent. Pilots fly the planes and helicopters. Cooks serve meals to the **exhausted** firefighters. Sometimes more than one thousand people work together at a fire. That's a lot of meals! The workers and firefighters all need each other to get the job done.

exhausted: *adj. very tired; worn out*

Celina was **exhausted** after working all day in the garden.

Sometimes more than one thousand people work together to help firefighters battle the blazes.

Damage Is Done

Articles like this one usually have a **main idea.** The main idea is the most important thing the writer is trying to say. The **facts** in the article help the writer explain the main idea. These facts are grouped into paragraphs. Each paragraph usually has a main idea, too. Sometimes the main idea is stated in the first sentence or two, but it does not have to be. It can be anywhere in the paragraph, even in the last sentence.

1. Underline the sentence that tells the main idea of the article.

    A Pilots are needed to fly helicopters.

    B Rangers watch for fires from lookout towers

    C Many people work together to fight fires.

    D Cooking for firefighters is hard work.

    ☑ Choices **A, B,** and **D** are facts that help explain the main idea. Choice **C** is the best answer because it is about all the details in the article.

2. If you could take a photograph to show people the main idea of the second paragraph, what would be in your picture?

    _____

3. Which of the sentences in the first paragraph under the head "Working Together" tells the main idea? Underline your answer.

    A First

    B Second

    C Third

    D Last

4. A head usually gives the main idea of part of an article. Find the head that says, "How Do Fires Start?" Then write a new headline for the paragraph.

    _____

5. Read the last paragraph of this article again. Then write what it says in your own words. In your answer, write the main idea and the details.

    _____

    _____

Sparks Fly

Root Words   Sometimes words that seem difficult at first are not as hard as they look. That is because many English words can be divided into parts. Each part has a meaning. The basic part of a word is called the "root." One of the vocabulary words in this passage is **unattended.**

> Sometimes all it takes is one spark from an *unattended* campfire to start a forest fire.

This word has the prefix *un-* and the suffix *-ed* added to the root word **attend.** To *attend* means to go to something. You *attend* school. The prefix *un-* means "not." When *un-* is added to *attended,* the word means "not attended." Here are some other words based on the root word *attend:*

attendance	attention	attentive

Use the forms of *attend* from above to fill in the blanks in the following sentences:

1. _____ all students! There will be a meeting today at lunch.

2. All students should _____ the meeting.

3. Mr. Brown will take _____ at the meeting.

4. Please be _____ when Mr. Brown is speaking.

Look at the list of words below. Each one has a prefix and/or a suffix. In the space next to each word, write the root word, and then use the first word in a sentence.

	Root	Sentence
1. dryness	_____	_____
2. hottest	_____	_____
3. traveler	_____	_____
4. impossible	_____	_____
5. uncomfortable	_____	_____
6. vacation	_____	_____

Mountain Madness

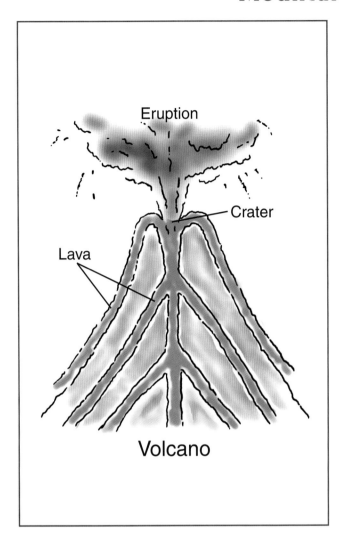

Volcano A volcano is an opening in the earth. Melted rock from inside the earth <u>escapes</u> through the opening. Usually volcanoes look like mountains. They are <u>located</u> all over the world—even under the ocean!

Lava Lava is rock that has melted from extreme heat inside the earth. Lava is the name for melted rock when it flows out of cracks in a volcano.

Crater A crater is a scooped-out place shaped like a bowl. Many volcanoes have craters at the top.

Eruption An <u>eruption</u> happens when rock, steam, and lava explode out of a volcano. The rocks break into pieces of different sizes. They can be very small pieces, or tiny <u>particles</u>. They can also be as big as houses. Some eruptions are very <u>destructive</u> to the area nearby.

Write the underlined words from the sentences above with their definitions below.

_____ *v.* found; placed

_____ *adj.* harmful; causing damage

_____ *n.* tiny bits; specks

_____ *v.* leaks out; gets free

_____ *n.* explosion; sudden bursting forth

The Mountain That Exploded

In May 1980, Mount St. Helens blew its top. One day the snow-capped volcano was covered with forests and lakes. The next day the trees were all dead, and the lakes were filled with mud and rocks. Everything for miles around was covered with a thick layer of ash. It was the most destructive eruption in the history of the United States. But it helped us learn more about volcanoes.

For over 100 years, Mount St. Helens in Washington looked like any other mountain. Most people forgot that it was really a sleeping volcano. They hiked on the trails. They fished in the lakes. They did not predict that the mountain would explode. But inside the mountain, something was happening.

Not *everyone* forgot that Mount St. Helens was a dangerous volcano. Two scientists who study the earth had been watching carefully. In 1975, they guessed that Mount St. Helens would erupt sometime in the next hundred years. They knew that deep in the earth the heat and **pressure** were building up. The melted rock was rising up into the mountain.

pressure: *n. force or strain of one thing against another*

Tony felt the **pressure** of the heavy pack on his back.

The Eruption

In March 1980, small earthquakes shook Mount St. Helens. Then there were explosions. Steam and ash began to escape from cracks. Soon the snow was gray. But this was not the eruption.

A lump appeared on the side of the mountain. It grew very large. Then on May 18, a bigger earthquake shook the lump loose. It tumbled down the mountain along with tons of rocks. This **violent** flow destroyed whole forests. It poured into Spirit Lake below and filled it with rocks and dirt. The mud, rocks, and dead trees sped down into the valley.

violent: *adj. caused by great physical force*

The dog's **violent** behavior scared many neighbors.

On May 18, 1980, a gigantic cloud of ash and gases shot out of the mountain.

The eruption of Mount St. Helens destroyed millions of trees.

Steam and rocks exploded from the hole where the lump had been. The rocks flew out at a very high speed. They knocked down many trees. Then the volcano erupted. Enormous clouds of ash and other particles rose high into the sky. The day grew very dark. Wind carried the ash far from the mountain. It fell in a thick blanket over forests and cities. Melted snow mixed with dirt and rocks raced down the mountain at 90 miles an hour!

After the Blast

The eruption lasted all day. It killed more than fifty people. It also killed thousands of animals and plants, and millions of trees. There was a giant crater where the peak of the mountain had been. Small amounts of lava and rocks came out of cracks in the crater for the next six years.

After the mountain cooled, bugs, birds, plants, and animals began to appear on Mount St. Helens. In some areas, paper companies planted trees. But the mountain does not look the same as it did before.

Mount St. Helens is still an active volcano. That means that it could erupt again. There are active volcanoes located all over the world. Scientists work together to watch these dangerous mountains. They measure the movement of the ground and study the gases that come out of the cracks. They look at pictures sent to earth from space. These scientists learned a lot from the eruption of Mount St. Helens. They cannot stop volcanoes from erupting. But when they think a volcano might erupt, they warn people living near the volcano to get away safely.

Comprehension

Lava Lesson

Sometimes the main idea is not written in a sentence. Then you must use the details to figure out what the main idea is. For example, look at the last paragraph in the article. A sentence telling the main idea might be, "Scientists study active volcanoes so they can warn people about future eruptions." That sentence is not in the paragraph. It combines some of the details in the paragraph to tell the main idea.

1. Underline the best headline for the second paragraph.
   A The Volcano Is Erupting
   B Scientists at Work
   C Danger Below
   D Hiking Can Be Fun

   ☑ Choices **A** and **B** are not stated in the paragraph. Choice **D** does not tell everything the paragraph is about. Choice **C** is the best answer.

2. Write a new sentence that tells the main idea of the second paragraph.

   _____

3. Underline the sentence that tells the main idea of the article.
   A Ash traveled far from the Mount St. Helen's volcano.
   B Bugs, birds, plants, and animals came back after the volcano cooled.
   C Scientists study the gases that come out of a volcano.
   D Mount St. Helens was the most destructive eruption in U.S. history.

   SEE PAGE 83 TO REVIEW TOPIC & MAIN IDEA

4. Write two details from the article that help explain the main idea.

   _____

   _____

5. Read the last paragraph again. Then write what the paragraph says in your own words. In your answer, include a main idea and details.

   _____

   _____

Molten Monuments

Prefixes are word parts attached to the beginning of root words to make new words. For example, the prefix *un-* means "not." When *un-* is attached to *safe,* it becomes *unsafe.* This new word means "not safe."

The area near Mount St. Helens was *unsafe* during the volcano's eruption.

It was *safe* for bugs, birds, plants, and animals to return when the mountain cooled.

Here are some prefixes and their meanings:

dis-	not
pre-	before
re-	again or backward

For each of the following words, choose a prefix from the list above to make a new word. You may use the same prefix more than once. *(Hint:* More than one prefix can be added to some words.)

Prefix plus root word

1. heat _____

2. appear _____

3. cycle _____

4. arrange _____

5. game _____

Now fill the blank in each sentence below with one of the words from above.

1. Before the team came on the field, the band did a _____ show.

2. We always _____ glass bottles instead of throwing them out.

3. The oven must _____ for ten minutes before we put the roast in.

4. We had to _____ the chairs to form a circle.

5. The magician made a coin _____ from his hand.

Andrew Attacks

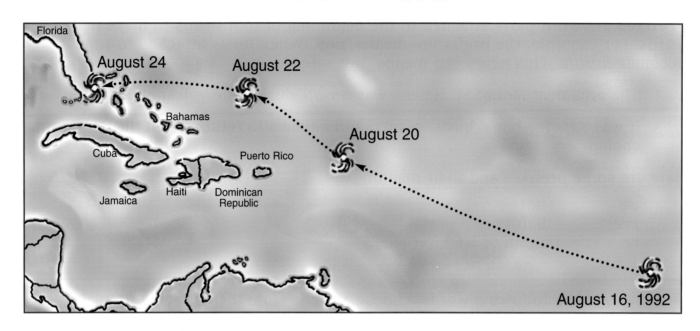

1. August 16, 1992. Weather watchers at the National Hurricane Center detect an area of wind and rain over the Atlantic Ocean. Scientists begin <u>tracking</u> it. They don't know what <u>direction</u> the storm will take.

2. August 20, 1992. The storm is 400 miles east of Puerto Rico. Scientists at the Hurricane Center study computer <u>data</u> about the storm.

3. August 22, 1992. Storm winds have reached 75 miles per hour. The storm is now officially Hurricane Andrew. The hurricane is <u>approaching</u> the East Coast of Florida. People living there are ordered to leave.

4. August 24, 1992. Hurricane Andrew strikes Florida with <u>fierce</u> winds.

> Read the information about the hurricane map. Then write the underlined word from above that matches each definition.

_____ *v.* moving close to; nearing

_____ *n.* path; course

_____ *v.* following the course or path of something

_____ *adj.* dangerous; powerful

_____ *n.* information, facts and figures

Path of Destruction

In the United States, we call them "hurricanes." In other parts of the world, they are called "typhoons," or "cyclones," or even "willy-willies." These are all different names for dangerous storms. These storms get started over the ocean. They grow larger and faster. If they hit land, they bring powerful winds, rain, and high tides. They also cause terrible destruction. And when they are gone, many people must work together to clean up the mess.

Hurricane Andrew hit Florida like a freight train.

Tracking the Storm

Scientists at the National Hurricane Center are very busy from May through November. That is "hurricane season" in the North Atlantic. The scientists study weather data. They look at photos taken from space. When they see a tropical storm growing, they give it a name. Then they can keep track of it. The first storm of the season begins with the letter A, the second starts with B, and so on. One year, for example, the first three storms were Alex, Bonnie, and Charley.

inland: *adv. away from the coast*

The weather is often warmer **inland** than it is at the beach.

On August 22, 1992, tropical storm Andrew reached hurricane force. Scientists could not be sure what direction Andrew would take, but they could make a good guess. They put out hurricane warnings for the coast of Florida. Many people packed up their things and headed **inland.** Others headed for shelters. But some people ignored the warnings. They stayed in their homes and waited as the storm approached.

Andrew Hits

In the middle of the night, Hurricane Andrew slammed into Florida. The main part of the storm hit two towns, Homestead and Florida City. The fierce wind threw mobile homes into the air. It tossed cars and trees around like toys. Power lines, telephone lines, and traffic lights were destroyed. Homes, stores, and schools were torn from the ground.

The people who had stayed in their homes were terrified. The wind speed reached more than 165 miles per hour. It blew windows into houses. It tore off roofs.

Hurricane Andrew left two cities in ruins.

Rainwater washed across floors. When the storm had passed through, Homestead and Florida City were in ruins. All of the buildings around Homestead Air Force Base were damaged. Over 250,000 people had no place to stay. Pets wandered lost in the streets.

The Cleanup

People in Homestead and Florida City had no homes, no water, and no food. They also had no electricity, no telephones, and no jobs to go to. It was still raining, and there were bugs everywhere. Soldiers in the National Guard came to help. They set up tents and kitchens. They **distributed** food and water. They guarded stores and homes. The Red Cross came, too.

> **distributed:** *v. handed out*
> The teacher **distributed** the new reading books.

Animal protection groups also came to help. They pulled horses out of the mud. They helped injured cats and dogs. They took care of the animals that had escaped from the Miami Zoo. Pet food companies sent thousands of pounds of food for the animals to eat.

During a hurricane, tree branches, telephone poles, and whole roofs can fly through the air like bullets. In just a few hours, entire neighborhoods can be completely destroyed.

All across the country, people heard about Hurricane Andrew. They sent food and clothing. They **donated** toys for children. Some came to help clean up the cities. Andrew was the most expensive storm ever to hit the United States. It took several years for all the damage to be fixed. In the end, it cost over 22 billion dollars to rebuild all the things Andrew had destroyed.

> **donated:** *v. gave*
> Ivan **donated** his book collection to the library.

Hurricane Help

Some details help make an article come alive but are not really needed to explain the main idea. For example, look at the first paragraph in this article. It is interesting to know that some people call hurricanes "willy-willies." But if you took this detail out, you would still understand the main idea of the article. Other details are more important.

1. Underline the sentence that tells the main idea of the article.

    A Pets can get lost in a hurricane.

    B Hurricanes are also called "typhoons."

    C Hurricanes cause terrible destruction.

    D Hurricane season is from May until November.

2. Read the second paragraph again. Then write what the paragraph says in your own words.

    _____

    _____

    _____

    _____

3. Look at the paragraph that follows "Andrew Hits." List two details in that paragraph that are important in explaining the main idea.

    _____

    _____

    _____

4. Write a new caption for the picture of the ruined cities that gives an important detail from the article.

    _____

5. Find the head that says "The Cleanup." In the first paragraph after this head, the main idea is not stated. Look at the details, and then write a sentence that tells the main idea.

    _____

    _____

Take Cover

Suffixes are like prefixes, except they come at the end of a word. When a suffix is added to the end of a word, the meaning of the word changes. When a suffix is added, sometimes the spelling of the word has to change. Here are some rules to follow:

1. If the word ends with an *e* and the suffix starts with a vowel, drop the *e*. For example, when the suffix *-ation* is added to *combine,* it becomes *combination.*

    Andrew was the most **expensive** storm ever to hit the United States.

    expense—expensive

2. When a word ends with the letter *y,* it is usually changed to an *i* before the suffix is added. For example, when the suffix *-ness* is added to *happy,* it becomes *happiness.*

    The people who stayed were **terrified.**

    terrify—terrified

Not all words follow these rules, but most do.

> Add a suffix from the list to each of the words below to make a new word. More than one suffix can be added to each word.

-ion	-ive	-ful	-less	-ment	-ly

1. care   _____   _____

2. act   _____   _____

3. thought _____   _____

4. protect _____   _____

5. detect _____   _____

> Add a suffix from the list to the word in parentheses to complete each sentence.

1. (excite)   There's always a lot of _____ before a storm hits.

2. (official) A storm is not _____ a hurricane until winds hit 75 miles per hour.

3. (home)   Strong storms may leave people _____.

4. (expense) Hurricanes can be very _____ storms.

5. (donate)   A _____ of food or clothing was welcomed after the storm.

Progress Check

✏ Choose words from the list to fill in the blank spaces.

located	escaped	rapidly	debris	fierce	eruption

Frozen in Time

Pompeii is located in southern Italy. It was once a busy town and favorite vacation spot for rich Romans. Today Pompeii still draws visitors. They wander through the streets, looking at maps and taking pictures.

Pompeii is frozen in time. Life stopped on August 24, A.D. 79 when Mount Vesuvius erupted one mile away. _____ streams of rock and ash began to pour _____ down the volcano. Some lucky people _____. When the _____ was over, thousands of people had died. Pompeii lay buried under 20 feet of ash.

In the 1800s, trained workers began to remove the _____ block by block. Art, jewelry, and household goods were perfectly preserved by their blanket of ash. Words written on walls could still be read. Shapes of bodies were _____ in the ashes. In a way, Pompeii had come back to life.

✏ How were the eruptions of Mount Vesuvius and Mount St. Helens alike and how were they different?

_____

_____

_____

_____

_____

Progress Check

✎ Compare the three natural disasters you have read about. Use information from this unit to fill in the chart below.

	Forest Fire	Erupting Volcano	Hurricane
What is destroyed?			
What causes the destruction?			
What can be done to prevent this disaster?			

✎ Which do you think is the most terrible natural disaster: a forest fire, an erupting volcano, or a hurricane? Explain your choice.

_____

_____

_____

✎ Briefly explain how people can work together to help in each of these emergencies:

a forest fire

_____

_____

an erupting volcano

_____

_____

a hurricane

_____

_____

Believe it or not!

- **Women in the United States could not vote until 1920. They fought for almost 100 years to get this right.**

- **Noise pollution has increased significantly in the United States. Loud noises, such as music at concerts, construction noise, and airplane noise, can lead to hearing loss, the number one disability in Americans.**

- **In 2001, a small car powered by gasoline and electricity was introduced. It will get 52 miles per gallon in city driving and 45 miles per gallon on the highway. In contrast, sport utility vehicles usually only get 12 to 16 miles per gallon.**

- **Individuals living in Alaska, Florida, Nevada, South Dakota, Texas, Washington, and Wyoming have no state income taxes to pay.**

- **Carbon monoxide is the number one air pollutant in the United States. Most of the pollution comes from forms of transportation.**

- **In 1971, the voting age for all United States elections was lowered from 21 to 18.**

Poll Position

The first Tuesday of November in the United States is election day. On that day <u>citizens</u> can choose new leaders for the government. They do this by going to a voting <u>site</u>. They can make their choice in a booth or write it on a <u>ballot</u>. But their <u>vote</u> is always private.

After the citizens vote for their favorite candidates, the votes are counted. The candidates who get the most votes are <u>declared</u> the winners.

Read the definitions. Write the underlined word from above which best fits each definition.

_____ *n.* the location of an event

_____ *n.* a piece of paper on which a voter marks a choice or choices

_____ *n.* people who live in a country

_____ *v.* to make known officially or with certainty

_____ *v.* to pick a candidate during an election

The Right to Vote

President Clinton is sworn into office.

When you are 18 years old, you will have the right to vote. American citizens can always express their opinions about the government. One way to do this is by voting for a candidate who has the same beliefs as you do. When you vote, you are helping to choose the leaders of your city, state, and country.

These leaders make decisions that matter to you and your family. The leaders decide how much money you have to pay the government in taxes. They decide how big your school will be and how much your teachers will be paid. They even decide how many days of school you'll have each year. As you can see, voting is an important task. If you choose not to vote, you are letting others decide your future for you.

Voting History

Voting in America has an interesting history. When the Constitution was written in 1781, only about six out of every 100 adult men were allowed to vote. Usually only rich white landowners could vote. In 1870, though, all men were given the right to vote. The Fifteenth **Amendment** to the Constitution said that all men could vote regardless of race or color. Fifty years later, women were given the right to vote, too.

amendment: *n. a change or improvement*

The Nineteenth **Amendment** to the Constitution gave women the right to vote.

People who fought to get women the right to vote, such as Susan B. Anthony and Elizabeth Cady Stanton, were called suffragists. These women used parades, silent protests, and speeches to get their point across.

None of these amendments came about easily. The women's rights movement began in the 1830s. The Nineteenth Amendment wasn't first introduced in Congress until 1878. It took more than 40 years for that amendment to be approved. People struggled for years so that everyone would have the right to vote. Even so, voter turnout in America is low. In 1996, only about half the adults in America voted in the Presidential election.

To Vote or Not to Vote

Why don't people vote? Some people think it is hard to vote. But polling places, where people vote, are usually easy to get to. They are located in schools, malls, and even in garages. Every polling place has people who can help new voters. Voters who can't get to a polling place can use an absentee ballot. They can fill out their absentee ballot before the elections and send it in by mail. Other people think their vote doesn't count. They are wrong; every vote counts. Sometimes elections are decided by just a few votes.

Closer Than Close

One of the closest elections in America was in 1948. President Harry S. Truman was running against Thomas Dewey. On election day everyone thought Dewey would be the winner. One newspaper was so sure Dewey would win that it printed the headline "Dewey Defeats Truman." But when all the votes were counted, Truman had won. Dewey received 45.1 percent of the votes. Truman received 49.5 percent.

President Truman celebrates after he, not Dewey, won the election.

The Presidential race of 2000 was an even closer election. Vice-president Al Gore ran against Texas governor George W. Bush. On election night, the television networks predicted Gore to be the winner in many states before the voting sites were closed. Later that evening, they changed their opinions and declared Bush the winner. Even later that night, they decided the numbers were too close to call.

President Bush is greeted by supporters.

The next day the country still did not know who had won the election. The state of Florida was so close that Vice-President Gore wanted a recount of votes. After many court rulings, the U.S. Supreme Court decided that there would be no recount of the votes. Governor Bush was declared the winner in Florida on December 13, 2000, thirty-six days after the election. That meant he won the vote in enough large states to be elected president.

Voting Matters

This article has many **details** about voting. The details give you information about the main idea of an article. They help you understand the main idea. You should be able to find the details in the article to answer these questions. Underline the correct answer to each question.

1. Before 1870, which of the following groups of people could vote?
   A all citizens born in the U.S.
   B all men who owned land
   C white men who owned land
   D all white men and women

   ☑ The correct answer is **C.** Reread the paragraph under the head "Voting History" on page 27. Read the third and fourth sentences where the correct details are given. The other answer choices give incorrect information; no details in the article support that information.

2. How can someone vote who will be out of town on election day?
   A by calling the polling place
   B by asking for help at the polling place
   C by waiting to hear if the election is close
   D by sending in an absentee ballot

3. Who won the presidential election of 1948?
   A Thomas Dewey
   B Harry S. Truman
   C George W. Bush
   D Al Gore

To answer this question, you must put details in the article together.

4. When did the Constitution give women the right to vote?
   A 1830
   B 1870
   C 1878
   D 1920

5. Write a sentence that tells the main idea of the article.

Count Me In!

Prefixes   A **prefix** comes at the beginning of a word and changes its meaning. For example, the prefix *semi-* means half. If *semi-* is attached to *annual,* it becomes *semiannual.* This new word means every half year or twice a year.

Here are some prefixes and their meanings:

micro-	small		*bi-*	two
multi-	many		*tri-*	three
tele-	distant		*semi-*	half

> For each of the following words, choose a prefix from the list above to make a new word. You may use the same prefix more than once. **Hint:** For some words, more than one prefix can be added. You should choose just one.

1. cycle   _____

2. level   _____

3. angle   _____

4. vision   _____

5. circle   _____

6. phone   _____

> Now use each new word in a sentence.

1. _____

2. _____

3. _____

4. _____

5. _____

6. _____

Tax Time

Some day you are going to have a career. You will earn an income for doing that job. Let's say your income is $1,000 a week. Does that mean you get $1,000? No. Your paycheck might be $720. What happens to the missing $280?

The answer is taxes. For every dollar you earn, you must pay taxes. A portion of everyone's paycheck goes to the government. We have to pay taxes in order to live in this country. Some of those deductions pay for many benefits from the national, state, and local governments.

Budget

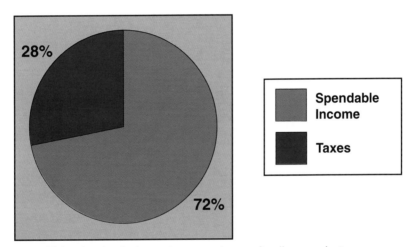

28%

72%

Spendable Income

Taxes

This pie chart shows how much one family pays in taxes.

Read the definitions. Write the underlined word from above which best fits each definition.

_____ *n.* a part of a whole

_____ *n.* the amount of money a person earns for a job

_____ *n.* things that improve life

_____ *n.* the amount of money taken out of one's paycheck

_____ *n.* part of one's income paid to the government

How Do Taxes Work?

There are many types of taxes. The first type is called income tax. You give the government some of your income—a portion of every dollar you earn. The amount the government takes is based on how much you earn. The more money you earn, the more tax you pay. Some people pay 15 cents for every dollar they earn. Other people pay 28 cents for every dollar. But almost everybody who earns money pays at least some income tax.

revenue: *n. total amount of money collected*

Julie used the **revenue** from her babysitting jobs to buy a CD player.

This may seem unfair. Why does the government get to take some of your money? Taxes are necessary to keep the country going. Tax **revenue** is used for many things. For example, if a hurricane or tornado occurs, the government uses tax money to help the people who were injured or left homeless.

Income tax is paid to the national government and the state government. Some cities, like New York City, even collect an income tax. In 1999, the national, or federal, government collected more than $800 billion in individual income taxes. That's a lot of money! But the money is used to take care of the American people. It helps pay for education, health care, military benefits and many other benefits.

A second type of tax is property tax. If you own a house, you pay a property tax. Property tax is based on the value of your house. This tax is paid to the local government. Property tax revenue pays to maintain the roads in your city. Without taxes, your town might not be able to pave streets or remove snow after storms. Property tax also pays for the police and fire departments.

Property taxes are used to help maintain the streets in your town.

$12.00

Another type of tax is sales tax. This tax is paid to state and local governments to fund even more services. Some states and cities have no sales taxes, but most do. The state or city decides how much sales tax to charge. When people buy things, sales tax is added to the price. Let's say you want to buy a $12 compact disk. You take the CD to the register, and the clerk says the price is $12.84. The extra eighty-four cents is for the sales tax. You don't have to pay sales tax on everything you buy. Food at the grocery store, for example, is usually not taxed.

Yet another tax is school tax. This is set by your local school district based on your property value. This tax helps pay for teachers' salaries, school renovations, and other school services in your local area.

Have You Paid Enough?

How do you know if you have paid enough taxes? First, you add up all the money you have earned that year. That number is your total income. Then you subtract any deductions. A deduction is an amount that is not taxed. A family with children, for example, can take a deduction. Parents can deduct some money for each child living in the house.

After you have subtracted all your deductions, the amount left is money on which you owe taxes. Every person or family must fill out a tax form. The form is sent to the section of the government called the Internal Revenue Service or IRS. The IRS determines whether you have paid enough taxes. If you haven't, you must send the extra amount with your tax form. If you get a **refund,** the IRS sends you a check in a few weeks or months.

refund: n. an amount of money given back to a person

The saleswoman gave John a **refund** when he returned the broken watch.

Taxes can be difficult to understand. That is why some people study tax laws in college and become accountants. They make a career of helping others do their taxes.

April 15 is an important date for all Americans. By that day, every person in the United States who made an income must fill out a tax form and send it to the IRS. The IRS makes sure that all individuals have paid their fair share of income taxes.

Pay to Play

You know that the main idea is about the entire article. Sometimes it is stated in the article, and sometimes it is not.

1. Underline the sentence that best states the main idea of the article you just read.

   A The IRS collects national income taxes.

   B Taxes pay for the services that the government provides.

   C Schools are supported by local and state taxes.

   D Sales tax is added to the price of items.

Details are important in an article, too. One type of relationship between details is **cause and effect.** This relationship shows how one thing causes or changes another. For example, if a person makes more money, he or she has to pay more money in taxes. The pay increase is the cause, and the tax increase is the effect. With that in mind, underline the answer to the following question.

2. To raise money for a new public playground in your city or town, the voters might approve an increase in the

   A property tax

   B income tax

   C sales tax

   D tax forms

SEE PAGE 86 TO REVIEW CAUSE AND EFFECT

    A new playground in your town will be funded by your local government. Choices **B, C,** and **D** are incorrect because these taxes are paid to the national or state governments. Only choice **A** is paid to the local government. So **A** is the correct choice.

3. Read the paragraph about buying a CD again. Finish this sentence:

   The $12 CD cost $12.84 because _____

   _____

4. Reread "Have You Paid Enough?" What is the effect of paying more taxes than you owe?

   _____

   _____

5. Look at the picture of the snowplow on page 32. Write a paragraph explaining how taxes make this possible.

   _____

   _____

   _____

Happy Endings

Suffixes   A **suffix** is added to the end of a word. It changes the word's meaning and its part of speech. When the suffix *-ness* is added to the adjective *happy*, the word becomes a noun, *happiness*.

> Katie is a *happy* baby.
> Katie has brought *happiness* into her family's life.

> Add a suffix from the box to change the words below into nouns. Use each new word in a sentence.

-ness	-ance	-ery	-dom	-ment

1. brave   _____

2. annoy   _____

3. excite   _____

4. free   _____

5. careless   _____

> Add a suffix from the box to change the words below into adjectives. Use each new word in a sentence.

-able	-al	-ive

1. practice   _____

2. act   _____

3. depend   _____

Earth Day

This is a picture of Earth from outer space. The oceans and rivers look blue. The land is brown and green. And a layer of white clouds covers parts of the planet. The Earth looks pretty and clean.

If you could take a closer look, you'd see that Earth isn't really so clean. Some of Earth's rivers and streams aren't blue at all. They are brown because they have been <u>contaminated</u>. Also, the clouds don't always look white. In some cities gasoline fumes <u>emit</u> a layer of dirty <u>smog</u> into the sky. Air <u>pollution</u> can make the sky and clouds look brown.

What can we do to help our <u>environment</u>? The first step is to learn what causes <u>pollution</u>. Then we can look at ways to help keep our Earth clean.

> Read each of the following definitions.

contaminate   *v.* to make unclean or impure

smog   *n.* a dirty layer of smoke and fog in the air

pollution   *n.* dirt and poisons in the air, ground, or water

environment   *n.* all the surroundings on Earth

emit   *v.* to give off or send forth

> Now write the word from above which best completes each of the following sentences.

1. Earth Day is a special day that reminds us to work to save our

   _____.

2. Oil spills _____ the oceans and can kill thousands of fish.

3. Factory smoke stacks _____ chemicals into the air.

4. One way to fight air _____ is to carpool to work or school.

5. The _____ was so thick that people could barely see the sun.

PROTECTING OUR ENVIRONMENT

Look carefully at the drawing above. At first, it seems like a normal neighborhood. However, there are several problems in this picture. The people are doing things that are hurting the environment.

Water, Water Everywhere

Water covers about 70 percent of Earth's surface. It may seem as though we could never run out of water. However, much of Earth's water is not safe to drink. Most of it is too salty for humans to drink. With about six billion people on Earth, we need a lot of water!

conserve: *v. to save or use carefully; to prevent waste*

The teacher asked her students to **conserve** paper by writing on both sides.

It is important not to waste clean water. People can **conserve** water by doing simple things. For example, we should make sure our sinks and pipes do not leak. We should not let the water run while we brush our teeth. We should be careful when we water a lawn. Look back at the drawing. Do you see how the sprinklers are wasting water? The grass needs water, not the sidewalk. We should be careful not to waste water.

But conserving water is not enough. We also have to keep the water clean. Who would want to drink a glass of contaminated water? Nobody. But animals and fish drink contaminated water every day. Sometimes factories are careless and let dangerous chemicals spill into lakes and streams. Farmers use chemicals to keep bugs from eating their crops. Those chemicals can find their way into the water, too. Oil spills are even more harmful. They happen when an oil tanker leaks oil into the ocean. Then millions of gallons of oil float on the ocean's surface. Oil can kill fish, birds, and other animals that live near seawater.

Oil spills contaminate oceans and kill animals.

There isn't much you can do to control a huge oil spill, but you can help to keep water clean. Look again at the drawing. Do you see the man changing the oil in his car? He is letting the old oil run into the storm drain. Those drains flow into rivers and oceans. The oil can harm plants and animals. The man could have saved the oil and taken it to a gas station where it will be thrown away properly.

Breathing Room

In some cities smog makes it hard for people to see and breathe.

refineries: *n. factories that remove unwanted matter from raw materials, such as oil, sugar, or metals*

The smoke from the sugar **refinery** filled the air with a sweet smell.

Clean air is just as important as clean water. *Smog* is a very common type of air pollution. The word *smog* is a combination of the words **smo**ke and **fog.** Smog is made when pollutants combine with the moisture in the air. The result is a thick layer of dirty air. Smog makes it hard to see and breathe.

One cause of smog is the burning of gasoline. Gasoline is the fuel that makes most cars, trucks, and buses run. Large cities are more likely to have smog because there are so many cars driving around. Another cause of air pollution is large factories and **refineries** with smoke stacks. They emit strong chemicals into the air. Here is one way the smog problem can be helped: people can use less gasoline. We can carpool to work or school. We can ride buses or subways. We can walk as much as possible or ride our bikes.

Gasoline is also used in lawn mowers, like the one in the drawing. The man in the picture is mowing his lawn at noon. The sun is still high in the sky. Scientists say it is best to mow your lawn in the morning or in the evening. Less gasoline fumes will rise into the air, and this will cause less smog to form.

There is only one Earth. It is everyone's responsibility to take care of it.

Wasting Away

The article you just read has a main idea and many details. The details give you information that supports the main idea. Sometimes the details are presented in order, or in a **sequence.** You need to follow the sequence as you read in order to understand the main idea. The words *first, then, next,* and *finally* can help you follow a sequence.

1. Read these sentences. Number the events in the order they happened.

   _____ **Next,** rain washes chemicals from the drops into a lake.

   _____ **Then,** the farmer sprays chemicals on the crops to kill bugs.

   _____ **Finally,** chemicals in the water cause harm to plants and fish.

   _____ **First,** bugs eat some of a farmer's crops.

   ☑ The two words *first* and *finally* tell you what events start and end the sequence. The words *then* and *next* also help you figure out the order. You can see that the farmer must spray the chemicals on before the rain washes them away. So the sequence is **3, 2, 4, 1.**

2. Rewrite the title of this article as a sentence. Your sentence should state the main idea of the article.

   _____

3. Explain how smog causes harm to the environment.

   _____

4. What is one thing you can do that will have a helpful effect on the environment?

   _____

5. Write three sentences to show the sequence of an oil spill as it is described in the article.

   First, _____

   Then, _____

   Finally, _____

Word Study

To the Ends of the Earth

Root Words   Some words that seem difficult to read are not as hard as they look. That is because many English words can be divided into parts. The basic part of a word is called the "root." Prefixes are parts of a word that come before the root. Suffixes come after the root.

Look at the list of words below. Each one has a prefix or a suffix added. In the space next to each word, write the root word.

refuel   _____   harmful   _____

wasteful   _____   careless   _____

conservation   _____

> Use a word from above to complete each sentence below.

1. Oil spills are _____ to animals that live near seawater.

2. It is _____ to run water while you are brushing your teeth.

3. A smaller car with good gas mileage allows you to _____ less often.

4. _____ of gasoline can help reduce smog.

5. Polluting rivers and streams is _____ and deadly to fish and plant life.

The word *form* is a common root word. Below are five prefixes and five suffixes. How many new words can you make by adding prefixes, suffixes, or both to the word *form?* Try to make at least five new words. Then use your new words or other combinations to fill in the blanks in the sentences.

Prefixes: *de-*   *in-*   *re-*   *trans-*   *uni-*

Suffixes: *-al*   *-er*   *-less*   *-ation*   *-erly*

New words: _____   _____   _____

_____   _____   _____

1. The police officer wore her _____ to work.

2. Please _____ your teacher if you know you will be late for school.

3. The students marched together in a perfect _____.

4. My father wore a tie and jacket to the _____ dinner party.

5. If we work together, we can _____ this empty lot into a lovely park.

Progress Check

✎ Choose words from the list to fill in the blank spaces.

portion	declared	pollution	citizens	contaminated	site

Deadly Oil

The largest oil spill in United States history happened on March 24, 1989. The oil tanker *Exxon Valdez* ran aground on a reef in Prince William Sound, Alaska. For two days, oil _____ the water. In total, 260,000 barrels of oil spilled into the _____. The cleanup was slow because companies involved were not prepared for the disaster. The oil slick coated a _____ of the Alaska shoreline and neighboring islands. Tens of thousands of birds were killed by the _____ in addition to thousands of sea mammals, such as sea otters. Alaska's important salmon crop was also damaged.

After more than 10 years, the _____ have _____ that the wilderness is on the mend.

✎ What were the negative effects of the *Exxon Valdez* oil spill described in the passage?

_____

_____

_____

_____

_____

Progress Check

✎ Write a sentence to describe what your responsibility should be to each of the following:

voting

_____

_____

paying taxes

_____

_____

protecting the environment

_____

_____

✎ Use what you have learned to finish the outline below. For each of the three headings, write words or phrases from the unit that tell when you can do it, why you should do it, and how doing it benefits society.

Voting

    when: _____

    why: _____

    how: _____

Paying taxes

    when: _____

    why: _____

    how: _____

Protecting our environment

    when: _____

    why: _____

    how: _____

UNIT 3

Describes The Brave People Who Explore New Lands

Have you ever traveled to a new place?
Put an X on any place you may have visited.

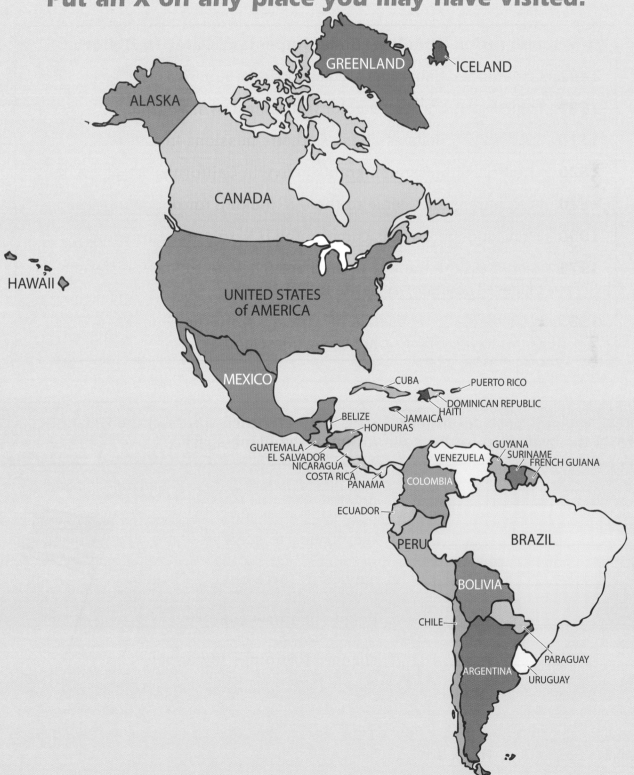

GREENLAND

ICELAND

ALASKA

CANADA

HAWAII

UNITED STATES
of AMERICA

MEXICO

CUBA

PUERTO RICO

DOMINICAN REPUBLIC

HAITI

BELIZE

JAMAICA

HONDURAS

GUATEMALA

EL SALVADOR

NICARAGUA

COSTA RICA

PANAMA

VENEZUELA

GUYANA

SURINAME

FRENCH GUIANA

COLOMBIA

ECUADOR

PERU

BRAZIL

BOLIVIA

CHILE

PARAGUAY

ARGENTINA

URUGUAY

43

A Nation of Hope

People come to the United States from all over the world. They hope to find a better life. Many come to find better jobs. Others come to live in freedom. Still others come to get a good education. Some people come for all of these reasons. They want to stay and become American citizens. These people are called immigrants. The United States has always been a nation of immigrants.

Immigration Timeline: Some Important Dates In History

1492 Christopher Columbus arrives in North America.

1607 English settlers start a colony at Jamestown, Virginia.

1770 Spanish colonists establish Catholic missions in California.

1820 The first Chinese immigrants arrive in California.

1840 Irish immigrants come to the U.S. looking for opportunities.

1950 Thousands of Cubans come to the U.S. to pursue freedom.

1975 People escape the war in Vietnam. They go to many different places. The majority settle in California.

1985 Wars displace thousands of Africans from their homes. Many come to the U.S. to find a new homeland.

Read each of these definitions. Using the underlined words in the timeline, write the best word for each definition in the blank space.

_____ *n.* most

_____ *v.* keep trying to achieve

_____ *v.* move out; force out

_____ *n.* people in a new country

_____ *n.* chances for things to happen

Annie's Special Day

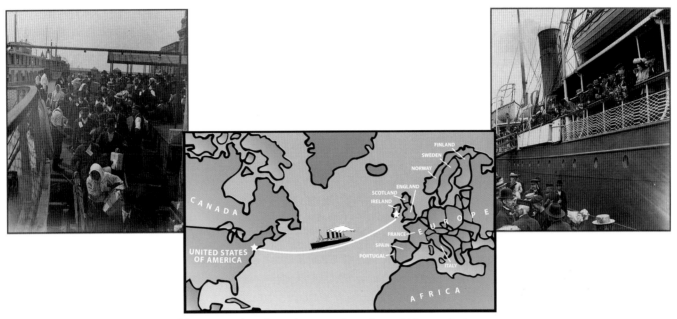

Annie Moore made a long journey from her old home to her new one.

For 50 years, people in Ireland had been suffering. A disease had killed almost all of the potato crops. Many people had starved to death. Others had to give up their farms. There were very few job opportunities. More than two million Irish were displaced. The majority left their homes for a better life in the United States during the potato **famine.**

> **famine:** *n. a lack of food; a time of great hunger and starvation*
>
> When the crops failed, there was a **famine.**

January 1, 1892 was an important day for Annie Moore. She and her two younger brothers, Anthony and Phillip, were about to arrive in the United States. They had traveled a long way across the ocean on a ship. They had come from Ireland to join their parents in New York City. Annie wondered what this new country would be like. Would there be enough to eat? Would there be jobs? Would her family have a better life?

Like many other Irish families, Annie's family had worked hard to immigrate to America. It had taken many years to save enough money. First, Annie's parents had gone to New York. It was very difficult for them to leave their children behind, but they knew they could make more money in America. They sent money back home. When they had saved enough and were able to establish a home, they sent for Annie and her brothers. Many immigrant families came to America this way. It was difficult for families to be split apart, but in those days, life in Ireland was worse.

The First Immigrant at Ellis Island

Annie didn't know that the day would be special in another way. She didn't know that her name would have a place in history. She stood on the deck of the boat and watched the island where they would reach the shore. She saw a big new building where many people were waiting for family and friends. Annie tried to spot her parents in the crowd.

Annie Moore was the first immigrant to come through Ellis Island.

Suddenly, Annie felt the boat bump into the island. People on the boat and on the shore gave a loud cheer. They had landed in America! Annie watched with excitement as the **gangplank** was lowered from the boat. In her hurry to find her parents, Annie was the first one off the boat. Annie skipped down the gangplank and was met by several important looking people who smiled and shook her hand. Then they walked with her into the big building.

gangplank: n. a board or ramp for people to walk from a ship to the shore

The cruise passengers walked down the **gangplank** to reach the island.

Inside the building, Annie and her brothers were reunited with their parents. They hugged and kissed each other. Her parents helped the children fill out important papers. Annie was now an immigrant to the United States. When they were finished, they listened to a man give a speech. He congratulated Annie. She was the first immigrant to come through Ellis Island, the new center for immigrants in New York. Then Annie was given a ten-dollar gold coin. It was the most money Annie ever had.

The Hard-Working Irish

In the years that followed, one million Irish followed Annie through Ellis Island. These poor Irish immigrants worked hard to bring their families to America. Like immigrants from many countries, they took the hardest jobs and the lowest pay. The men and boys helped to build railroads and dig coal. The women and girls worked in factories making cloth out of cotton and silk.

Through their hard work, many Irish-Americans became successful. They became educators, writers, and business people. Some became leaders, like John F. Kennedy and Ronald Reagan, two presidents of the United States. Like Annie Moore and her family, many Irish immigrants faced hardships to become Americans.

Big Changes

Stories like this one tell things like names, places, and dates. For example, *Annie Moore* was *the first immigrant to come through Ellis Island.* She came from *Ireland* in *1892.*

Other things are not clearly stated. You have to think about them. When you do this, you **infer** things from the article. You can infer that Annie's parents missed her, even though the article doesn't say so. When Annie saw her parents again, *they hugged and kissed each other.*

1. Which of these statements tells something you can *infer* from the story? Underline the best answer.

   A Annie Moore's face was shown on one side of the ten-dollar gold coin.

   B Annie Moore became an American citizen the day she arrived.

   C The speech Annie heard was about the opening of Ellis Island.

   D The picture of Annie Moore was shown in the New York newspapers.

    You can eliminate **B** because immigrants must follow certain rules before they become citizens. **A** cannot be true because officials did not know who would be the first person to get off the boat. **D** may be true, but there is nothing in the story to suggest that Annie's picture was in the papers. Answer **C** is the best answer. Since Annie was the first immigrant to go through Ellis Island, it makes sense that the speech was for the opening of the center.

2. Read the first paragraph of this story. Underline the answer that is the best inference from information in the paragraph.

   A Potatoes are an important source of nutrition.

   B In the 1800s, most people in Ireland were farmers.

   C People who came to America from Ireland were starving.

   D The population of Ireland in the 1800s was two million.

3. Find the paragraph under the heading "The First Immigrant at Ellis Island." Read it again. Make an inference. Underline the word which best tells what Annie became that day.

   A Angry

   B Famous

   C Lost

   D Beautiful

4. Write a sentence that tells what you think Annie's life was like in Ireland before she came to America.

   _____

   _____

New Arrivals

Homonyms are words that sound the same but have different meanings. They are also spelled differently. The words *ate* and *eight* are homonyms. Jorge **ate** seven or **eight** cookies. These words look very different and mean different things, but they sound exactly the same. There are many homonyms in the English language.

> Read the sentences below. Write the correct homonym in the blank in each sentence.

1. The immigrants were excited to _____ (meat/meet) their new American friends.

2. After many years of war in their country, they came to the United States to find _____ (peace/piece).

3. The _____ (plane/plain) ride was long, and the immigrants were tired.

4. One suitcase held all of the family's _____ (close/clothes).

5. Even though life would be hard, they were very happy to be _____ (hear/here).

> Now write 5 new sentences. In each sentence use one of the homonyms from above that you did NOT use in the blanks above. The first one is done for you.

1. The immigrants from Peru made a stew with meat for the party. _____

2. _____

3. _____

4. _____

5. _____

> In the blanks after each word, write a homonym for the word. Some of these words have two homonyms. Write one of them on the line.

1. buy _____   3. write _____

2. weight _____   4. sail _____

"Mobile Home" of the Pioneers

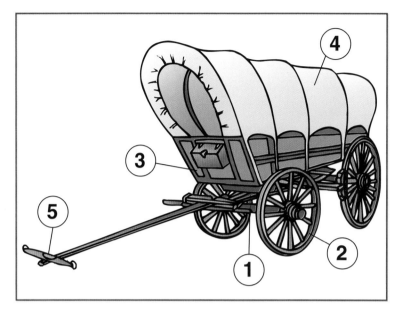

Covered wagons are famous in American history. As pioneers moved West, many traveled in a covered wagon called a "prairie schooner" (SKOO•ner). A schooner is a kind of large ship. Some people thought that covered wagons looked like ships traveling on land instead of water. That's how they got the name.

1. The <u>sturdy</u> wooden base of the wagon was made from thick, heavy pieces of wood. The undercarriage had to be strong. The pioneer trails were almost always rough and bumpy.

2. The wheels were also made from wood. A flat iron "tire" fit over the rim. Nails <u>connected</u> the iron tire to the rim to protect the wood.

3. The wagon box held most of the pioneers' things. The box was about three feet deep. Cracks between the boards were filled with tar to <u>protect</u> the goods in the wagons from getting wet.

4. The best-known part of the prairie schooner was the cloth top. It was called the "bonnet." It was usually made of cotton <u>material</u>. The heavy cloth was sometimes painted with oil to help keep out the rain.

5. Most prairie schooners were pulled by mules or oxen. Mules could go faster, but oxen were cheaper. The oxen could also survive harsh weather better than mules. Still, pioneers often had to <u>abandon</u> their wagons in bad winter storms.

Read the sentences below. Choose one of the underlined words above to fill each blank.

---

1. Sports clothes should be made of a strong _____.

2. A bike helmet will _____ your head from injury.

3. You need to be strong and _____ to play football.

4. The crew had to _____ the sinking ship.

5. The two mountain climbers were _____ by a rope.

Trail of Courage

Most of western North America was unknown land to the white settlers.

It was early May in the year 1841. People were getting ready to leave Missouri. They were planning to make new homes in the western **territory.** They had a long, long way to travel in their sturdy prairie schooners. The trip would take about five months.

territory: *n. area of land*

Before Oregon became a state in 1859, it was called the Oregon ***Territory.***

On a hill outside of Independence, Missouri, the first wagon train got ready. Toward the west there was plenty of wide-open land. There were few trees and no buildings or people. There were no roads. There wasn't even a trail!

Many pioneers did not know what would happen on the trail.

The leader of the wagon train, John Bidwell, was a teacher and a farmer. He didn't know anything about the wilderness, and he didn't have a guide to show the way. Still, the settlers were ready to get started. It was hard to make a living in Missouri. They had heard there was good land in California and Oregon where they could have their own farms.

Of course, Native Americans had lived in the west for thousands of years. A few European explorers and trappers had already crossed the **continent.** They had opened many different trails, but they didn't travel in heavy wagons loaded with supplies. And the European explorers and trappers rarely traveled with small children. No covered wagons had crossed the country before 1841.

continent: *n. a giant piece of land on the earth*

Each *continent* on the earth has a name: Africa, Antarctica, Asia, Australia, Europe, North America, and South America.

Good Luck and Bad Luck

The pioneers had to travel across flat land, through rivers, and over mountain regions.

At first, the Bidwell wagon train had good luck. After just a few days on the trail, they met another group going west. This group had a guide, a mountain man whose name was Tom Fitzpatrick. For the first half of the journey, the two groups traveled together. They followed the Platte River across the flat land. There was plenty of water to drink and grass for the horses and oxen. The early days on the trail were easy.

Soon, however, the wagon train had to leave the river. The pioneers had to go north through the Rocky Mountains. Now it became harder to travel. Wagons sometimes broke down. Water and firewood material were harder to find. People and animals were tired. Because of Fitzpatrick's help, they made it halfway to the west.

At a place called Soda Springs, Fitzpatrick left to go in a different direction. Some of the Bidwell pioneers wanted to go on to Oregon. The rest wanted to keep on going to California. The two groups decided to split up. Now there was no one to guide and protect them. Still they went on.

Soon the weather began to change. Winter was coming. Supplies began running low. Some of the travelers got sick. Wagons broke down. One by one, the pioneers had to abandon their prairie schooners and continue on foot.

These pioneers were determined to survive. They would not quit. By the end of October, they had reached California and Oregon. They had very sore feet, but they had succeeded! Their success gave more pioneers the courage to move west.

If you travel to Oregon, you can learn more about the pioneers and wagon trains at the "End of the Trail" Museum in Oregon City.

During the next 24 years, thousands of people traveled on the pioneer trails. They all faced great hardships. But each year the trails grew easier to follow. Over time, the wagons wore tracks in the earth. In some places you can still see the tracks of the prairie schooners connecting the grassy plains. They remind us of the courage of the early western pioneers.

New Journeys

The following questions ask you to **infer** something. Remember, when you make an inference, you figure out something that is not actually stated in the article. You must think about what *is* stated to infer, or figure out, things that are not written.

1. Look at the map at the beginning of the article. Read the first paragraph again. Then write two reasons why the pioneers' journey would be dangerous.

2. Name four things the pioneers probably took on their journey.

Underline the answers to the following questions.

SEE PAGE 88 TO REVIEW
DRAWING CONCLUSIONS & MAKING INFERENCES

3. You can infer from this article that the first wagon train included mostly
   A fathers
   B cowboys
   C families
   D teachers

4. The pioneers were probably most in danger in
   A April
   B June
   C August
   D September

5. Why did more and more pioneers decide to go west after the events in the article took place?
   A They wanted to see the wild animals.
   B They were forced to leave the east.
   C They wanted to meet John Bidwell.
   D They heard about the first successful trip.

Pioneer Power

Synonyms are words that have the same meaning. *Fast* and *quick* are synonyms. They mean the same thing. Either word is correct in the following sentence:

*Jamie is a good soccer player because she is very **quick**.*
*Jamie is a good soccer player because she is very **fast**.*

Read the sentences below. Choose the best synonym for the underlined word.

---

1. John needed special tools to <u>repair</u> the broken wagon wheel.
   A turn
   B push
   C fix
   D paint

2. After thousands of pioneers traveled over the Oregon Trail, the route became more and more <u>popular</u>.
   A hidden
   B difficult
   C dangerous
   D well-known

3. Pioneers had to be brave, strong, and <u>clever</u> to survive the dangers of the trail.
   A rich
   B smart
   C famous
   D handsome

4. To arrive before winter, the wagon train had to move more <u>rapidly</u>.
   A carefully
   B slowly
   C quickly
   D quietly

Think of as many synonyms as you can for each of the words below.

---

1. thin _____   3. near _____

2. happy _____   4. see _____

To the Moon

The moon may be the site of the first space <u>colonies</u>.

1. The <u>fuel</u> needed to send heavy equipment to the moon is costly.

2. This kind of spaceship will <u>launch</u> humans to the moon.

3. Here is one idea for a house in the lunar colony.

4. People will <u>survey</u> the moon in lunar rovers.

5. Moon colonists will do <u>experiments</u> on the land before returning to Earth.

colonies	*n.*	the new place where groups of people settle
experiments	*n.*	tests done to find out something
fuel	*n.*	a substance that is burned to give off heat or energy
launch	*v.*	to send upward
survey	*v.*	to look over or examine

> In the following sentences, fill each blank with the correct word from the list above.

1. The new _____ were built quickly by the hard-working people.

2. They did _____ to find the best materials to build homes.

3. Neil Armstrong was the first to _____ the moon's surface in person.

4. NASA has plans to _____ spacecraft to the moon.

5. They will use a new _____ that is not harmful to the atmosphere.

Which Way to Mars?

A settlement on Mars could be a real possibility in the near future. Why go to Mars? Just as Christopher Columbus and Lewis and Clark did so long ago, there is interest in exploring new lands.

It won't be easy to get to Mars. The "Red Planet" is far away from Earth. It would take years for spaceships to go there and come back. There is another problem. A trip to Mars will be very expensive.

What makes it so expensive? A spacecraft is heavy. The fuel it needs will cost a lot of money. Lighter spacecraft need less fuel. Scientists have been looking for ways to make spacecraft lighter so that travel to Mars won't cost so much.

What Is the Best Plan?

One scientist, Robert Zubrin, has a plan he calls "Mars Direct." It would cost less than most other plans and would also be safer. Zubrin says that we already have the technology we need to get to Mars. Here's how his plan would work.

international: *adj. all over the world*

The Internet makes **international** communication easy.

In the first year, the United States and its **international** partners would launch a rocket from Earth. The rocket would fly into space carrying an ERV, or Earth Return Vehicle. High above the Earth, the rocket will "throw" the ERV to Mars. The ERV is the key to the Mars Direct plan.

Human missions to Mars would allow astronauts to search for signs of life on the planet. Under the Mars Direct plan, new missions would occur every two years.

There will be no people on the ERV. Instead, it will carry all the things necessary for people to live on Mars. After the ERV lands on Mars, scientists on Earth will control it. They will use the ERV to set up a camp for the humans. Equipment in the ERV will be able to make oxygen and water.

How an ERV might look blasting off from Mars

Will Mars Be Safe for Humans?

Two years later, two more rockets will be launched from Earth. One will carry another ERV. The other will carry a crew of four people and a special house for them to live in. The people will bring enough food and supplies to last three years. They will also bring a ground rover they can drive on Mars.

How a colony on Mars might look

According to Zubrin, people will be safe on Mars. The ERVs will make oxygen for them to breathe. The ERVs will also make water for them to drink. The special house will have a kitchen, bedrooms, bathrooms, and even an exercise room. There will be a lab for experiments and a library for reading and studying.

The crew will stay on Mars for a year and a half. They will use their ground rovers to survey the planet and perform experiments. They will also prepare the planet for the next Mars mission. When their time is up, they will use the ERV to return to Earth.

How a support system for a Mars colony might look

Many scientists believe that people will live on Mars in the future. Robert Zubrin hopes it will happen soon. Zubrin thinks it is important to explore space. He believes we should build colonies on the Red Planet. And, he hopes that his Mars Direct plan will make it possible.

Mission to Mars

Many times you must think about what you read and then tell what you think will happen in the future. You will make a **prediction.** Your prediction should be based on information in the article.

SEE PAGE 90 TO REVIEW MAKING PREDICTIONS

1. According to the article, which of these might happen in the future? Underline your answer.

   A ERVs will be made heavier than other spacecraft.

   B The Mars Direct plan will save money.

   C Robert Zubrin will go to the moon.

   D It will be easy to build a colony on Mars.

   ☑ Choice **A** is incorrect because it is stated in the article that spacecraft need to be lighter in the future to use less fuel. Choices **C** and **D** are also incorrect. Robert Zubrin wants to build a colony on Mars. Even he says the plan will be difficult. Therefore, only choice **B** is correct. If Zubrin's plan is carried out, it will cost less than other plans.

2. Underline the sentence that tells why the ERVs are the key to the Mars Direct plan.

   A They will stay in outer space.

   B Humans won't have to control them.

   C They will get Mars ready for humans.

   D Humans will leave them on Mars.

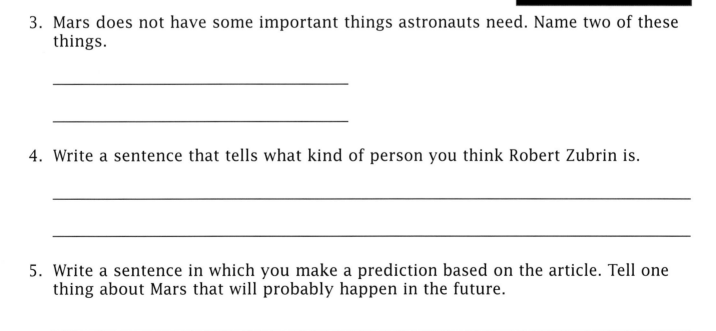

3. Mars does not have some important things astronauts need. Name two of these things.

   _____

   _____

4. Write a sentence that tells what kind of person you think Robert Zubrin is.

   _____

   _____

5. Write a sentence in which you make a prediction based on the article. Tell one thing about Mars that will probably happen in the future.

   _____

   _____

Stop or Go

Antonyms are words that have opposite meanings. For example, *fast* and *slow* are antonyms.

The rocket to Mars will travel very **fast.**

The Mars Direct plan will be **slow** to accomplish because it is expensive.

> Write an antonym for each of the following words:

1. weak _____

2. same _____

3. last _____

4. tall _____

5. loud _____

> Change the meaning of each sentence by crossing out the underlined word and writing its antonym on the line.

1. Ira would not swim in the <u>shallow</u> water.   _____

2. Beth <u>cried</u> when she heard the story.   _____

3. The climber reached the <u>bottom</u> of the mountain.   _____

4. I am thinking of an <u>even</u> number greater than one.   _____

> Circle the two words that are antonyms of each other in each sentence.

1. Carla wore her old black coat and her new blue jeans.

2. Micah and his sister found the money that their father lost under the sofa.

3. Jake forgot to pack his lunch, but he remembered to bring money with him.

4. Juanita tried to act friendly when she walked past the large, mean dog.

Progress Check

✎ Choose words from the list to fill in the blank spaces.

displace	materials	opportunities	colonies	pursue	territory

Don Juan de Oñate

Who were the first Europeans to establish permanent settlements in North America? Most people think it was the English soldiers who settled in Jamestown, Virginia, or the Pilgrims who landed in Plymouth, Massachusetts. But before the Jamestown and Plymouth settlements, there were _____ of settlers from Spain in the Southwest.

The Spanish had already settled in Mexico. But Spain did not want to send explorers into unknown areas. A Spanish *conquistador* named Don Juan de Oñate was so sure there were _____ for wealth to the north that he agreed to pay for a trip himself. In 1598, Oñate crossed the Rio Grande River into what is now the state of New Mexico. Oñate did not come alone. With him were missionaries from Spain and some 200 soldiers with their families. They brought their animals and wagons filled with _____ to build new homes. Oñate had furnished everything. His band of people and animals was over four miles long!

The Spanish colonists did not intend to _____ the Native Americans from their homes. In fact, the new settlers made friends with the Indians. They lived together peacefully for many years. But Oñate was not a good governor. He was greedy and wanted to _____ his own wealth. Over time there were problems between the Spanish and the Indians. For a short time, the Indians drove the Spanish out, but the colonists returned. The colony was occupied by the Spanish and by Indians for over 100 years before Mexico reclaimed the _____.

✎ In what ways was Don Juan de Oñate a good leader?

_____

_____

Progress Check

✎ Compare Don Juan de Oñate's journey to that of the first people who will visit Mars. Use the information from this unit and the passage about Don Juan de Oñate to fill in the chart.

	Alike	Different
Don Juan de Oñate		
Travelers to Mars		

✎ Write a sentence that compares one similarity and one difference between Don Juan de Oñate and the travelers to Mars.

_____

_____

✎ What are three changes that immigrants face when they come to the United States?

1. _____

2. _____

3. _____

UNIT 4

Highlights Some Of The Choices You Have Now And In The Future

Many people who come to the United States from other countries become United States citizens. You will read about why some people choose to come here and the process they go through to become a citizen.

You will read about Sammy Sosa's childhood in the Dominican Republic and why he chose to come to the United States to play baseball.

The homes of the future will be very different from the homes of today. You will have many choices to make for safety features and convenience. Computers will power most of these smart homes through voice command.

Special Guest

On November 11, 1998, 86 immigrants from 31 countries stood in front of a judge in Washington, D.C. They were there for a special ceremony. They were becoming citizens of the United States. A special guest was there, too. The guest was Madeleine Albright, the United States Secretary of State at the time. The Secretary of State does not usually go to these events. However, this date was of exceptional importance to Dr. Albright. It marked the 50th anniversary of the day she and her family became residents of the United States.

When people come to this country, they do not automatically become citizens. They must live here for five years. They must learn about United States history and pass a test. Then they must promise to be loyal to the United States. Dr. Albright spoke about the time when her family first came here. She said the United States "was generous enough to welcome us, make us feel at home, and allow me to grow up in freedom. For that, I will always be grateful." Madeleine Albright rose to one of the most important jobs in our country. She is a fine example of how much opportunity people have in the United States. That is why each year there are many applications for citizenship to the "land of the free."

Read each of these definitions. Write the best word for the definition in the blank space. Use the underlined words from the story.

_____ *n.* people who live in a place

_____ *adv.* done right away without need for thought or control

_____ *n.* a formal act in honor of an event or special occasion

_____ *n.* written requests

_____ *adj.* faithful in support of a person, country, or cause

Madeleine Albright gives a speech.

★ ★ ★ Becoming a Citizen ★ ★ ★

Not everyone who lives in the United States is a citizen. People who are born in the United States are automatically citizens. But some people come to the United States from other countries. They are immigrants, or residents, but not citizens. An immigrant is a person who is allowed to live in this country without being a citizen. An immigrant must follow certain steps to become a citizen.

Why Become a Citizen?

People come to live in the United States from other countries for many reasons. Some people come to live with their family members. Others come because they can find better jobs here. Still others come because they want freedom that they do not have in their own countries.

Citizen—person born in the United States or born to U.S. citizens in foreign countries.

Naturalized Citizen—person born in another country who has become a citizen of the United States.

Alien—person who has come to the United States from another country.

Most people who come to the United States to live want to become citizens. Some adults want to be citizens so their children will be citizens. United States citizens have many rights and privileges. One of the most important is the right to vote. Citizens elect the president and the other people who run the government. Immigrants cannot vote. Immigrants cannot be elected to office either.

How Can an Immigrant Become a Citizen?

Suppose you have just arrived in the United States, and you want to become a citizen. The first thing you must do is become a "legal permanent resident." That means you can stay here. You must live in the United States for five years as a legal permanent resident, and you must be 18 years old, before you can apply for citizenship.

You begin by filling out an application for citizenship. You must send your application to the government with your fingerprints and three pictures of yourself. Then you can take the citizenship test. This test asks questions about United States history and government. There are 20 questions, and you must get at least 12 questions right in 30 minutes. If you don't pass the test, you can take it again, as many times as you like.

interview: *n. meeting of people face to face*

I had an **interview** with the manager for my new job.

The next step is the citizenship **interview.** During the interview, a government official looks over all your papers and asks you questions. You must show in the interview that you can speak, read, and write some English. You may also have to answer more questions about U.S. government and history.

The Last Step

The last step in the process of becoming a citizen of the U.S. is taking the "Oath of Allegiance." This oath is like the Pledge of Allegiance. An "oath" or "pledge" is a promise, and an "allegiance" means loyalty. When you take the oath, you promise to be loyal to the United States and not to another country. After the ceremony, a judge grants you citizenship. At last you receive a certificate that shows you are a citizen of the United States of America.

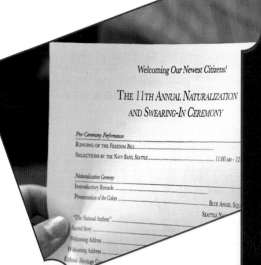

Welcoming Our Newest Citizens!

THE 11TH ANNUAL NATURALIZATION AND SWEARING-IN CEREMONY

Pre-Ceremony Performances
Ringing of the Freedom Bell.......
Selections by the Navy Band, Seattle.......................11:00 am - 12

Naturalization Ceremony
Introductory Remarks.......
Presentation of the Colors.......................BLUE ANGEL SQ...
"The National Anthem".......................SEATTLE N...
Sacred Story.......
Welcoming Address.......
Welcoming Address.......
Ethnic Heritage C...

OATH OF ALLEGIANCE TO THE UNITED STATES OF AMERICA

"I hereby declare, on oath, that I absolutely and entirely renounce and abjure all allegiance and fidelity to any foreign prince, potentate, state or sovereignty, of whom or which I have heretofore been a subject or citizen; that I will support and defend the Constitution and laws of the United States of America against all enemies, foreign and domestic; that I will bear true faith and allegiance to the same; that I will bear arms on behalf of the United States when required by the law; that I will perform noncombatant service in the armed forces of the United States when required by the law; that I will perform work of national importance under civilian direction when required by law; and that I take this obligation freely without any mental reservation or purpose of evasion; so help me God."

No Ordinary Oath

When you read an article, you learn many details. You also put the details together to draw conclusions about the information in the article. The conclusions are your own understanding of the article. Underline the answers to questions 1–4 below.

1. Which of these is a conclusion that you can draw from reading the article?

    A It takes at least five years to become a citizen.

    B Children become citizens before their parents.

    C In order to become a citizen, a person must vote.

    D Immigrants come to the U.S. from many countries.

     A is the best choice. According to the article, an immigrant must be a legal resident for five years, so it must take at least that long to become a citizen. Although answer **D** is true, there is no information in the article that helps you draw that conclusion. The other answers are not true.

2. From the part of the article "Why Become a Citizen?" you can conclude that

    A all immigrants who come to the United States want to become citizens

    B families usually come to the United States together

    C an immigrant can always get a job in the United States

    D when immigrants become citizens, their children become citizens, too

3. During a citizenship interview, the interviewer wants to find out

    A where the immigrant has come from

    B if the immigrant has filled out the application

    C if the immigrant will be a good citizen

    D whether the immigrant has a job

4. Immigrants take the Oath of Allegiance to show that they

    A promise to be loyal to their new country

    B can speak and read English

    C know the history of the United States

    D have completed all the steps

5. Why do you think a person must be at least 18 to become a citizen, and a citizen must be at least 18 to vote?

_____

_____

Building a Life

Root Words   **State** is the root word of **statement** and **restate.** The words in the left column below are root words. Match prefixes or suffixes from the center column to create new words. You may have to change the spelling. Then use your new words to fill in the blanks in the sentences below.

locate

govern

reside

re-

-ion

-ment

-ent

_____

_____

_____

_____

1. The mayor of a city is part of the local _____.

2. We moved to a new _____ in another city.

3. Jake is a _____ of New York City.

4. My family decided to _____ so we could live closer to our school.

Add a prefix or a suffix to each of the following words. Some roots can take a prefix and a suffix. Then write a sentence for the new word.

1. Root: require   New word: _____

   Sentence: _____

2. Root: fill   New word: _____

   Sentence: _____

3. Root: correct   New word: _____

   Sentence: _____

4. Root: able   New word: _____

   Sentence: _____

5. Root: employ   New word: _____

   Sentence: _____

Sammy Sosa Timeline

1968 Sammy Sosa is born in the Dominican Republic.

1975 Sammy Sosa's father dies <u>unexpectedly</u>.

1986 Sosa goes to the U.S. for the first time to play for a minor league team.

1989 Sosa joins the Texas Rangers. He is later traded to the Chicago White Sox and then the Chicago Cubs.

1990 In Sosa's first full season as a major league player, he hits 15 home runs.

1995 Sosa hits 36 home runs in the regular season (before the playoffs).

1997 St. Louis Cardinals' first baseman, Mark McGwire, hits 58 homers; Sosa hits 36.

1998 Mark McGwire, in <u>competition</u> with Sosa, hits 62 home runs.

1998 Sammy Sosa receives the National League's Most <u>Valuable</u> Player award, an important personal <u>accomplishment</u>.

2000 Sammy Sosa received the Hispanic Heritage Award for his <u>talent</u> on and off the field.

Read each of these sentences and fill in the blanks with one of the underlined words from the timeline.

1. There were ten teams in the gymnastics _____.

2. Finishing that long book was a major _____ for Nick.

3. My grandparents were surprised when we _____ rang their doorbell.

4. The notes Jackie took were _____ in helping her study.

5. Playing the violin in the community orchestra takes a real _____.

Slammin' Sammy

In the summer of 1998, the name Sammy Sosa became a household word. This twenty-nine-year-old Chicago Cubs baseball player was in the headlines of newspapers around the world. How did this young man from the Dominican Republic unexpectedly gain fame? He and St. Louis Cardinals' first baseman Mark McGwire were in a friendly competition. They both were trying to break a very old baseball record.

In 1961, the New York Yankees' Roger Maris hit a record 61 home runs in a single season. Thirty-seven years later, Sosa and McGwire finally broke Maris's record. When all was said and done, McGwire ended the regular season with 70 home runs. Sosa was not far behind with 66. Sammy Sosa did not win the home run race. However, he helped his team make it to the playoffs, and he won the National League's Most Valuable Player (MVP) award. He also won the hearts of people all over the world, especially in his home country of the Dominican Republic.

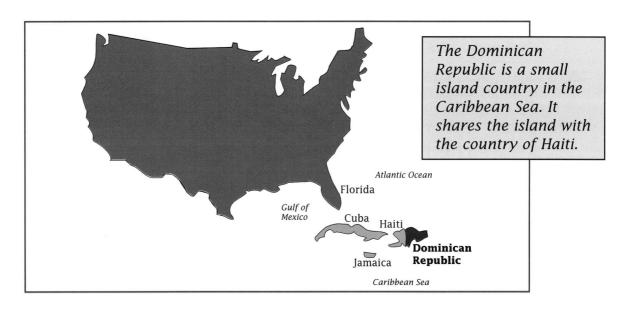

The Dominican Republic is a small island country in the Caribbean Sea. It shares the island with the country of Haiti.

Opportunity Knocks

The events of the summer of 1998 were a far cry from Sammy's childhood. As a boy in the Dominican Republic, Sammy worked hard to help his family make ends meet. When his father died, his mother was left alone to raise five boys and two girls. Sammy helped out by selling oranges, shining shoes, and washing cars. Much of the time Sammy and his friends played baseball on dirt streets. They didn't have gloves, so they would catch the balls with their hands. They often used a rolled-up sock for a ball and a stick for a bat. Sammy didn't start playing baseball on a real team until he was 14 years old.

When Sammy was just 16, baseball scouts from the United States started to notice his talent. At 17, he came to the U.S. for the first time to play ball on a minor league team. At the time, he spoke no English! Over the next few years, Sammy worked his way up in the major leagues, but he never lost sight of his family back home in the Dominican Republic. He made money to support his family. Baseball was his way to help his family.

Big Mac and Slammin' Sammy

Sammy Sosa was not selfish. He learned quickly how much it meant to be part of a team. Sammy believed that his most important accomplishment in 1998 was helping his team get to the playoffs. Reporters asked Sammy about the **pressure** of the home run race with Mark McGwire. He said, "Pressure is shining shoes and washing cars to support my family in the Dominican Republic." He explained that now he went to bed happy every night and was very thankful to have the chance to play ball in the United States.

> **pressure:** *n. a situation or event that causes concern*
>
> The **pressure** of having to do a report in front of the class made me nervous.

Sosa and McGwire shared the spotlight through the 1998 season. McGwire was known as "Big Mac" and Sosa was called "Slammin' Sammy." McGwire matched Roger Maris's record of 61 homers before Sosa did. However, Slammin' Sammy was not jealous. When the Cubs met the Cardinals in their final game of the season, Big Mac hit homer number 62, breaking Maris's record. Even though Sammy was chasing the same record, he ran from his position in right field to give his buddy a big hug of congratulations. It was a proud moment for Mark McGwire and St. Louis Cardinal fans.

A New Home

Sammy Sosa found a new home in the United States. Through baseball he has made a good life for himself and his family. But he hasn't forgotten his roots. Sammy still visits the Dominican Republic. He also helped raise money for his country after a hurricane. No wonder Sammy Sosa is beloved by two countries!

Keeping His Eye on the Ball

This article includes information about Sammy Sosa. Use the information to **draw conclusions** that help you understand the whole article. Remember that a conclusion is based on information. Underline the answers for 1–3 below.

1. Which of these is a conclusion you can draw from information in the article?

    A As a child, Sammy Sosa played baseball with his father and brothers.

    B Baseball scouts found Sammy because he was playing on a team.

    C Mark McGuire hit more home runs than Sammy Sosa in 1998.

    D Sammy had to learn English before he could play baseball in the U.S.

    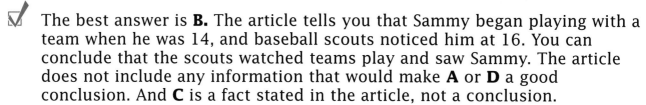

    The best answer is **B.** The article tells you that Sammy began playing with a team when he was 14, and baseball scouts noticed him at 16. You can conclude that the scouts watched teams play and saw Sammy. The article does not include any information that would make **A** or **D** a good conclusion. And **C** is a fact stated in the article, not a conclusion.

2. The nickname "Slammin' Sammy" probably refers to

    A Sammy slamming his car door

    B the position Sammy plays

    C how hard Sammy hits the baseball

    D how long Sammy practices each day

3. When Sammy hugged Mark McGuire, he showed that he was

    A happy for his friend

    B covering up his anger

    C tired of trying to win

    D jealous of McGuire

4. Sammy Sosa could not speak English when he came to America. How did that probably have an effect on his early baseball career?

    _____

    _____

5. How did Sammy Sosa's childhood prepare him to be part of a team?

    _____

    _____

Beyond Baseball

Idioms   You can't understand the meaning of an idiom from the meaning of the individual words. For example, "There's no reason to cry over spilled milk" is an idiom. It means, "Don't get upset over things that are not really that important." It is not really about milk at all.

In this article, the heading before the third paragraph, "Opportunity Knocks," is an idiom. It means that someone is being given a chance at something. Here are some other sentences from the story with idioms. The idioms are underlined. Rewrite each sentence in your own words, replacing the idiom. A sample is done for you.

Sample: In the summer of 1998, the name of Sammy Sosa became <u>a household word</u>.

In the summer of 1998, the name of Sammy Sosa became familiar to most people.

1. <u>When all was said and done</u>, McGwire ended the regular season with 70 home runs.

   _____

2. He also <u>won the hearts</u> of people all over the world, especially in his home country of the Dominican Republic.

   _____

3. The events of the summer of 1998 were <u>a far cry</u> from Sammy's childhood.

   _____

4. Sammy worked hard to help his family <u>make ends meet</u>.

   _____

5. He never <u>lost sight of</u> his family back home in the Dominican Republic.

   _____

Here are some other common idioms and what they mean.

Idiom	Meaning
Up the creek without a paddle	*In trouble*
Let the cat out of the bag	*Tell a secret*
At a snail's pace	*Very slowly*
Promise the moon	*Promise something impossible*
Burn the midnight oil	*Stay up late to work or study*

The Home of the Future

In the home of the future almost every <u>appliance</u> will be run by computers. People will tell computers what to do with a voice <u>command</u>. And there will be computers to perform many tasks for people. One <u>device</u>, for example, will send a signal to you that the mail has arrived. Other devices will be used for <u>security</u>. You will be able to program lights to come on at different times. Flood lights will <u>illuminate</u> a driveway or a backyard when someone walks by the light. Most of these inventions will make life easier and safer for homeowners.

Read each of these definitions. Write the best word for the definition in the blank space. Use the underlined words from the story.

_____ *n.* a piece of equipment

_____ *n.* a piece of equipment, such as a toaster or a stove, designed for a specific task

_____ *v.* to give orders to; direct

_____ *v.* to shine light on

_____ *n.* safety; something to help make things safe

It's Your Life!

There are many ways to live in the United States. People live in cities and suburbs, in trailer parks and on farms. You will have to decide how you want to live someday. You will have many choices. Will you choose to live in an apartment or a house? Will you drive a car or take buses and trains? Will you work at home or in an office? Here are two very different ways to live today.

A Simple Home

Some people live without many of the things that you use every day. In parts of the United States, Amish people live a very simple life. They live near one another and work on farms. Children walk to school. Their houses do not have electricity, and they do not drive cars or trucks. Their homes are heated with stoves, and they read by daylight or lamplight.

The Amish do not use any electronic appliances such as vacuum cleaners or dishwashers. They sweep their floors and wash dishes and clothes by hand. They hang clothes outside to dry in the wind. Kids in the family help with all the farm and house chores. Of course, there are no television sets or computers in an Amish home. People read books and newspapers and make many things. Children play with simple wooden toys.

A "Smart" Home

Most homes today use tools and appliances that make life easier. Computers and other electronic devices control many of these machines. Having a home with all these devices is called "automation." Automation makes it possible for people to do more things. Automated machines do a lot of the work that people used to do. These machines make the coffee, wash and dry the clothes, and open the garage door for us.

The word automation *is a combination of the words* automatic *and* operation.

"Smart" homes are houses with many electronic devices that make using automated machines even easier. Remote control devices, such as the one for your TV, and keypads will mean that you don't even have to touch an appliance to make it work! You might be in your bedroom ready to go to sleep. Then you remember that you forgot to turn your computer off. All you do is punch in numbers on the keypad on your wall. The computer is turned off.

Many electronic devices are used for security. In some smart homes, lights turn on when someone comes to the front door. A **sensor** illuminates the driveway as soon as a car drives up. An alarm sounds when a window or door is broken. If a fire starts while the owners are away, an automated home will not only call the fire department, it will also alert the neighbors and even turn on the sprinklers.

Every day there are new inventions that will make life easier and safer. Someday, you will be able to give directions to your appliances with a voice command. For example, you could call your home from school and tell the oven to turn itself on to 350 degrees for 10 minutes. Or you might have a sensor in your mailbox. Perhaps you don't want to go out in the rain to see if there is mail. The sensor sends a signal to tell you that there is mail in the box.

Which of these devices do you think you will live with? Or will you decide on a simple life where you do things for yourself?

What a Way to Live!

1. This article tells about two ways of living. Compare them to see how they are alike. What things can you think of that both kinds of homes must have? Write at least five things.

   Simple Home   vs.   Smart Home

   _____

   _____

   _____

   _____

   _____

2. How would your life be different if you lived in an Amish home? What would be different for you at each of these times?

   in the morning _____

   after school _____

   in the evening _____

3. Which of these can you conclude from reading this article? Underline your answer.
   A Computers are being used in creative ways to make our lives easier.
   B Builders are looking for new ways to make homes cost more.
   C The home of the future will have a computer in every room.
   D Cooking and cleaning will no longer be necessary in the future.

   SEE PAGE 88 TO REVIEW DRAWING CONCLUSIONS & MAKING INFERENCES

4. List two ways that smart homes make using automated machines even easier.

   _____

   _____

5. The article gives many examples of automation in homes. Think of another example that may be possible in the home of the future. Write a sentence telling how it would work.

   _____

   _____

Room with a View

Multiple Meaning Words   When a word can have more than one definition, we say that it is a **multiple meaning word.** For example, *blue* is a multiple meaning word. We can use it to describe a color, as in a *blue* sky. We can also use it to mean sad, as in feeling *blue.*

> The words in the left column below appear in the article you just read. Each word has multiple meanings. The meaning of the word as it is used in the article is written next to it. Draw a line to the definition in the right column that is another meaning for the word.

Design	make a plan for	hit with a fist
Play	take part in	move fast
Punch	press to operate	pattern of shapes or lines
Run	function or control	period of time
Term	word with a certain meaning	story acted out on stage

> Here are some other words from the article that also have multiple meanings. Each one fits into two of the sentences below. Fill in the blanks with the words that fit in these sentences.

call	cold	fire	still	bright

1. When the teacher wants to ask a student a question, she will _____ the student's name.

2. Sunglasses help protect our eyes from the _____ sun.

3. The employee did not do her work, so the boss had to _____ her.

4. The class sat very _____ during the program.

5. Be sure to dress in warm layers when it is _____ outside.

6. The house is on _____!

7. Joe's quick answers showed the teacher that he was a _____ student.

8. I'm coughing a lot because I have a _____.

9. If you need help, give me a _____.

10. Although it is September, the weather is _____ hot.

Progress Check

✎ Choose words from the list to fill in the blank spaces.

valuable	devices	loyal	residents	competition	ceremony

Another Way of Life

The Amish are a religious group who live in settlements in 22 states and in Ontario, Canada. The oldest group of Old Order Amish live in Lancaster County, Pennsylvania. What makes the Amish unique is that they choose to get along without modern _____.

The _____ of the Amish community all drive horses and buggies rather than cars, do not have electricity in their homes, and send their children to private one-room school houses through only the eighth grade. After that, they work on their family's farm or business until they marry. The wedding _____ is also important to the Amish because family is the core element in the Amish church.

Amish women wear long dresses made from solid-color fabrics with long sleeves and an apron which are fastened with straight pins or snaps. They never cut their hair. The women do not own _____ items or wear jewelry. Amish men also wear dark-colored suits and solid-colored shirts. They wear suspenders and wide-brimmed black or straw hats. The men grow long beards without mustaches when they marry in place of wearing a wedding ring.

The Amish are not in _____ with each other or the outside world. They follow simple beliefs and work together as _____ community members to help each other.

✎ Compare a modern house and what you know about an Amish house. List three things not mentioned in the passage that the Amish probably do not have in their homes.

_____

_____

_____

Progress Check

✎ What are the steps that Sammy Sosa must go through if he wants to become a citizen of the United States?

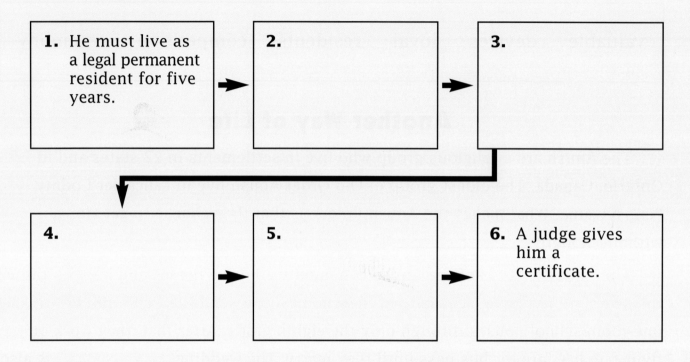

1. He must live as a legal permanent resident for five years.

2.

3.

4.

5.

6. A judge gives him a certificate.

✎ Think about the three articles you read in this unit. Write a sentence that explains one thing that is given up in each of the articles.

Becoming a Citizen

_____

_____

Sammy Sosa

_____

_____

It's Your Life!

_____

_____

Posttest

Write the root word of each of these words.

abandonment   _____   unexpected   _____

conservative   _____   automatically   _____

eruption   _____   deductions   _____

relocated   _____   residential   _____

extremely   _____   amendment   _____

competition   _____   contamination   _____

Use one of the prefixes or suffixes below to write a new word. Then write
a sentence using the new word.

re-	pre-	-ful	-ion

destruct   _____

_____

appear   _____

_____

school   _____

_____

success   _____

_____

celebrate   _____

_____

cheer   _____

_____

The Oldest Rookie

The story of Jim Morris' baseball career is the stuff dreams are made of. Morris had always wanted to pitch in the major leagues. In January 1983, he was drafted by the Milwaukee Brewers while he was in junior college. The left-handed pitcher played on and off in the minor leagues until 1989 when elbow and shoulder injuries forced him to give up his dream of playing baseball forever—or so he thought.

A Comfortable Life

After his six years in the Minor Leagues, Morris returned to school to get a teaching degree. He settled in to a comfortable job teaching science and coaching baseball at Reagan County High School in Big Lake, Texas.

> *To learn more about the Major Leagues, go to* **www.mlb.com**

Jim had worked hard to turn the Reagan Owls into a winning team. In the three years before he arrived, the team had never won more than three games in one season. One thing that made the players improve was trying to hit their coach's pitching in practice. They complained that he threw too hard. One day Jim struck out most of his players at batting practice. The team and Morris made a bet. If the Owls reached the playoffs that year, the coach would try out for a major league baseball team. Morris "lost" the bet.

That summer Morris attended a Tampa Bay Devil Rays' tryout camp. He showed up with his baseball glove and his kids. Morris joked to the baseball scout why he was there. But without even warming up, he consistently threw pitches at 90 miles-an-hour and faster. The Devil Rays recognized his pitching talent immediately and signed him to the organization as a relief pitcher. Morris rose through the minor league in just three months and was promoted to the big leagues on September 18, 1999. Jim Morris had become the oldest rookie to play in the major leagues since 1970. He was 35 year old! His first time on the mound, Morris threw a 96 mile-an-hour fast ball to strike out a batter with just four pitches.

Inspiration and Injuries

Many people call Jim Morris an inspiration, but Jim says he never stopped to think about it. He did not read the papers or watch television reports about himself. He just tried to live the dream that his wife and players urged him to follow. "In May, I was signing report cards," Morris said with amazement. "Now I'm signing autographs."

Morris continued to pitch with the Devil Rays until injuries to his left elbow forced him to have surgery. The team released him after he was on the injured list for most of the 2000 season. Then the Los Angeles Dodgers invited him to attend their camp that winter. Jim practiced for a few months, then decided to retire from baseball rather than risk permanent injury to his left elbow and shoulder.

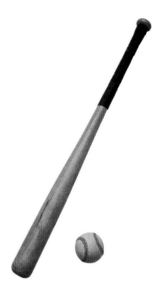

Far From Over

Although his major league baseball career was a short one, Jim Morris is not at all disappointed. In fact, he says he is still amazed that his dream came true. And he credits the kids he coached for encouraging him to reach for his goal. But that's not the end of Jim Morris's story! His autobiography, *The Oldest Rookie,* was published in April 2001. His life story is being made into a movie. The film called *The Rookie* began shooting in May 2001. Jim's perseverance and success will continue to inspire others.

An autobiography is a story of a person's life written by that person.

Posttest

1. Underline the main idea of the article you just read.
   A Major league baseball did not appreciate Jim Morris's talent.
   B Jim Morris did not like teaching science.
   C Jim Morris returned to professional baseball after 10 years.
   D Jim Morris wanted to make a movie about his life.

2. Why did Morris's high school team think he should try out for major league baseball? Underline your answer.
   A His pitching was as good as a professional baseball player.
   B He was not a good baseball coach.
   C The team wanted to go to the state playoffs.
   D They wanted him to make good on the bet he lost.

3. Why did Morris retire from baseball after only two years in the major leagues? Underline your answer.
   A He wanted to return to teaching.
   B He had a chance to star in a movie about baseball.
   C He thought he was too old.
   D He did not want to keep injuring his arm.

4. Why is Jim Morris considered an inspiration?

   _____

   _____

5. List the events of Jim Morris's baseball career in sequence.

A	He was drafted by the Milwaukee Brewers in 1983.
B	
C	
D	
E	
F	

Topic and Main Idea

Any passage you read is *about* something. That's true whether it's a paragraph, a chapter, or a whole book. There's a **topic** that the passage is about. There's a **main idea** that's most important to the topic. Other details in the passage support the main idea.

PAGE 83 REVIEWS TOPIC & MAIN IDEA

> Read this paragraph. Identify the topic and find the main idea.

Su and Alison were going to be a horse for Halloween. They had planned the costume in April and worked on it since July. Now the costume was finished. They were in Su's living room, ready to try it on.

This paragraph is *about* Su and Alison's Halloween costume. That's the **topic.** The first sentence tells the **main idea.** The other sentences all help explain this main idea.

In many paragraphs (but not all), the main idea is expressed in a **topic sentence.** It's usually (but not always) the first or last sentence in the paragraph.

> Underline the topic sentences in these paragraphs. On the line below each paragraph, write a few words explaining what the topic is.

What is the most-visited museum in the world? That honor goes to the National Air and Space Museum in Washington, D.C. It's located on the National Mall, between the United States Capitol and the Washington Monument. It's open every day except December 25. Admission is free.

Topic: _____

One exhibit at the museum explains how things fly, from balloons to rockets. Another lets you pilot a plane to a landing. Of course, you're really flying a computer. There are historic films showing the role of aircraft in peace and war. You can see why you'll want to come early and stay all day!

Topic: _____

> What is the topic of the whole passage? Write a title that expresses its main idea.

_____

Facts and Details

Facts and details in a passage help you understand the main idea better. They support and explain the main idea. They answer questions like *who, what, where, when,* and *how.*

> You've already identified the topic in the paragraph below. The main idea is underlined. Look for facts and details that help you understand the main idea.

Su and Alison were going to be a horse for Halloween. They had planned the costume in April and worked on it since July. Now the costume was finished. They were in Su's living room, ready to try it on.

1. How long had they been planning the costume?   Since April

2. What was happening?   They were going to try the costume on.

3. Where were they?   In Su's living room

All these details and others help you to better understand the main idea.

> Read the passage below. The sentences that express the main idea in each paragraph are underlined. Answer the questions about facts and details that support the main idea.

The first skateboards were really homemade scooters. This was in the early 1900s. Kids would take the wheels off roller skates and fasten them to boards. They would mount a wooden crate on the front of the board. They attached handles to the crate for better control.

A few daring and foolish riders took the crates off their boards. But true skateboards did not come along until the 1950s. The sport of surfing was then becoming popular in California. Some surfers discovered that a board with wheels gave a ride like a surfboard. Surfboard makers began to make and sell skateboards in 1963. However, the wheels on these early boards were made of clay. They did not grip the road well.

1. When were the first skateboards made? _____

2. What were they made from? _____

3. How did surfing lead to the first true skateboards? _____

4. When were skateboards first made for sale? _____

5. What kind of problem was there with these boards? _____

_____

Sequence of Events

The **sequence of events** in a passage is the order in which things happen. Usually, but not always, events or steps are named in order. Usually, but not always, there are clue words that help you identify the order.

PAGE 85 REVIEWS SEQUENCE OF EVENTS

> Here is a 2,600-year old recipe from an ancient Greek cookbook. Note the order of steps.

Mix 1 cup flour, 1 cup water, and 1 tablespoon honey in a bowl. Beat until they form a batter. Next, heat 2 tablespoons cooking oil in a pan. Then pour about a fourth of the batter into the hot oil. Turn two or three times until evenly brown. Cook three more pancakes the same way. Before serving, pour honey over them and sprinkle with sesame seeds.

Watch for time clues that mark the sequence. In this paragraph, words like *next, then,* and *before* are time clues. Dates, days, and hours can also be time clues.

1. Mix flour, water, and honey.
2. Heat oil.
3. Pour batter into hot oil.
4. Keep turning until cooked.
5. Pour on honey and sesame seeds.
6. Serve.

> Read a passage about author Maya Angelou. Then use the numbers 1 through 10 to list important events of her life in order.

Most people know Maya Angelou as an author and poet. She published her first book in 1970 and her first book of poems in 1971. But she is also a performer, teacher, and producer. She toured Europe as an actress and singer in 1954. She first performed on the New York stage in 1957. She first danced professionally when she was 17. From 1962 to 1964, she lived and worked in Africa. She became an expert on African cultures. In 1974, she produced a series about Africa for American television.

Maya Angelou was born in St. Louis, Missouri in 1928. She grew up in Stamps, Arkansas and San Francisco, California. In 1959, she moved to New York City. She has lived in North Carolina since 1998.

_____ She published her first book.

_____ She published her first book of poems.

_____ She toured Europe as a singer.

_____ She first acted on the New York stage.

_____ She first danced professionally.

_____ She lived and worked in Africa.

_____ She produced a TV series about Africa.

_____ She was born in St. Louis, Missouri.

_____ She moved to New York City.

_____ She moved to North Carolina.

Cause and Effect

Events happen for a reason. These "why?" connections between events are called **cause-and-effect** relationships. The *effect* is the thing that happens. The *cause* is the reason that it happens. Sometimes you have to read carefully to see cause and effect.

PAGE 86

REVIEWS

CAUSE AND EFFECT

Read the paragraph below. Pay attention to causes and effects.

Joel's mom had to work late that week. So Joel had to get supper for his young sister. Since he had to be home, he missed swimming practice all week. Because he hadn't worked out, he wasn't sharp for Friday's meet and lost his race by a second. "Blame it on Mom's boss," he grumbled.

This table shows causes and effects in the paragraph. Note how words such as *so, since,* and *because* are clues to the reasons that things happen.

Cause	Effect
Joel's mom had to work late.	Joel had to get supper for his sister.
He had to be home.	He missed swimming practice.
He hadn't worked out.	He lost his race.

Now read this paragraph. Fill in some causes and effects in the table below.

The Grand Banks is an area of shallow sea off the Atlantic coast of Canada. A cold current crosses the banks. A warm current runs along the eastern part. The mixing of the two currents makes the Grand Banks a rich environment for plankton. Fish come to feed on the plankton. As a result, the Grand Banks is one of the world's best fishing grounds. In fact, the Grand Banks has been overfished. That's one reason catches have been much lower in recent years. Another is pollution, which harms plankton.

Cause	Effect

Compare and Contrast

Often as you read, you sort out information about how items are similar and different. When you note what's similar about two or more items, you're **comparing** them. When you note what's different between them, you're **contrasting** them.

Read about Jon and his brother Tim. Note what's alike and different about them.

Jon and Tim both like music. Jon plays the guitar, while his brother's instrument is the violin. Both boys like ice cream. Jon's favorite flavor is chocolate and Tim's is vanilla. Neither one watches TV much.

The diagram at the right is called a *Venn diagram.* It organizes the information to help you compare and contrast Jon and Tim. Note how words like *both, while, and,* and *neither* are clues to what's similar and different about them.

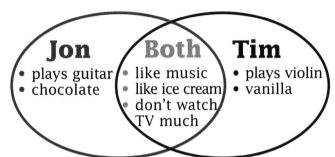

Jon
• plays guitar
• chocolate

Both
• like music
• like ice cream
• don't watch TV much

Tim
• plays violin
• vanilla

Now read about our two most famous presidents. Compare and contrast them by organizing the information in a Venn diagram. Then fill in the table below.

George Washington and Abraham Lincoln are both ranked among our greatest presidents. Washington led our country during its first years, while Lincoln led it during its most troubled years. Both were tall men. Lincoln had black hair and wore a beard. Washington had red hair and was clean-shaven. Washington was a soldier and a land surveyor, while Lincoln was a lawyer. Both their pictures are on our coins and bills.

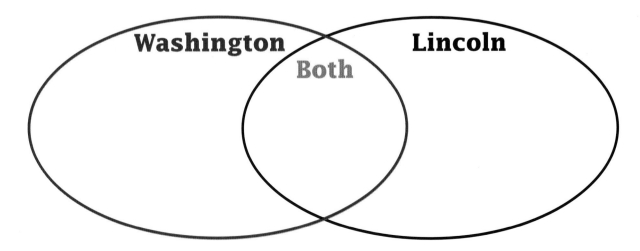

Washington   **Lincoln**

Both

Drawing Conclusions and Making Inferences

Authors don't always state facts directly. Sometimes you have to figure them out yourself from other details. This is called **drawing conclusions.** Sometimes you can figure things out from what you already know. This is called **making inferences.**

Read a passage about a girl named Zhing. Draw conclusions and make inferences to figure out some facts that are not stated in the passage.

Zhing leaned on her hoe. She held a hand to her forehead and squinted in the bright sun. Far across the fields rode a column of soldiers on horseback. They wore armor, despite the hot sun. They were moving at a steady pace toward the Great Wall.

You can guess several things this passage doesn't tell you. The tone of the paragraph tells you that it's fiction. *The Great Wall* suggests that it takes place in China. *Soldiers wearing armor* tell you that it's set in the past. And *the hot sun* tells you that it's summer.

Now read a paragraph about an animal. Draw conclusions and make inferences to answer the questions at the bottom of the page.

There are two species of mongoose. One is native to India, the other to northern Africa. Both have slender bodies up to two feet long and are covered with gray or brown fur.

Mongooses in the wild eat rodents and snakes. They are famous for their attacks on large poisonous snakes. Their quick, twisting movements allow them to avoid being bitten. They are easily tamed and are often kept as pets to control snakes. They have been brought into many countries for that purpose. However, it is illegal to bring mongooses into the United States, as they might kill helpful animals.

1. Is a mongoose a reptile, mammal, or bird? _____

2. What other animal is about the same size as a mongoose? _____

3. Can a mongoose die from a snake's poison? _____ How can you tell?

_____

4. People keep mongooses to control snakes in the same way that they keep

_____ to control _____.

5. What kind of helpful animals might mongooses kill? _____

_____

Fact and Opinion

Don't believe everything you read! Not all nonfiction is fact. Some of what you read is opinion—the author's or someone else's. Can you tell the difference? A **fact** can be proven. An **opinion** is what someone thinks, feels, or believes. It cannot be proven.

Read a student's book report. Write **F** before each sentence that states a fact. Write **O** before each sentence that states an opinion.

Wayside School Is Falling Down is by Louis Sachar. It's one of the funniest books you'll ever read. Wayside School is 30 stories tall, and there are 30 "stories" in the book. They're mostly about the kids in Mrs. Jewls' class. Anyone who goes to school will recognize these kids. The book tells the truth about what school is like. But it tells it in very odd ways.

Did you put an **O** before the second sentence and before each of the last three? The other sentences are facts. You could prove them by reading the book. Judging words like *funniest* and *truth* are clues to opinions. So are generalizing words like *anyone.* They signify what someone believes. But they are not facts.

Read an article from a school newspaper. Then write **F** or **O** beside the sentences below to tell whether they are facts or opinions.

Our school needs a new electrical system. It still has the original wiring from 1955. It's OK for running light bulbs and slide projectors. But it's not good enough for the computer age. Our classroom has only two computers. Everyone wants to use them all the time. But the wiring in place now can't handle any more than two. We think the PTA should raise money for a new electrical system. In today's world, you can't learn without computers.

_____ 1. Our school needs a new electrical system.

_____ 2. It still has the original wiring from 1955.

_____ 3. But it's not good enough for the computer age.

_____ 4. Our classroom has only two computers.

_____ 5. Everyone wants to use them all the time.

_____ 6. But the wiring in place now can't handle any more than two.

_____ 7. The PTA should raise money for a new electrical system.

_____ 8. In today's world, you can't learn without computers.

Making Predictions

As you read, you're often **making predictions.** You use clues from the passage combined with what you know to guess what's going to happen.

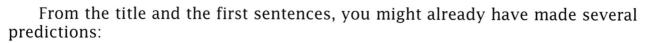

> Read the first paragraph of a story called "Night Sweats." Predict what will happen. Use clues from the passage combined with what you know about folktales.

> *There's no such thing as a vampire,* Aaron told himself. Still, the old house looked like something out of a Dracula movie. And why had the woman in the Post Office looked at him that way when he asked directions to the old Klassen place? *I'm only going to be here a week,* Aaron thought. *Stupid to believe in fairy tales.*

From the title and the first sentences, you might already have made several predictions:

- *Something scary is going to happen to Aaron.*
- *This isn't going to be a realistic story.*
- *There's going to be something in it about blood.*

You make predictions when reading nonfiction, too. You use clues from the passage combined with what you know to make good guesses about people and future events.

> Read the first part of an article about a scientist. Make predictions to answer the questions at the bottom of the page.

> Sometimes science is like detective work. One of the greatest detective scientists was Louis Pasteur. He became fascinated with microscopic life forms. His experiments looked into their connection with diseases. The result was probably the most important medical discovery of all time.

> Pasteur was born in France in 1822. When he was a boy, a boy in his town was bitten by a wolf. The wolf had rabies, and the boy died. No one then understood what rabies was, let alone how to prevent it.

1. What do you think Pasteur's "most important medical discovery" was?

_____

2. List three more things that you would expect to read about in this article.

_____

_____

_____

Glossary

abandon: *v.* to leave because of danger
We had to abandon the burning house.

accomplishment: *n.* something carried out; an achievement
Making the gymnastics team is quite an accomplishment.

amendment: *n.* a change or improvement
The 19th Amendment to the Constitution gave women the right to vote.

appliance: *n.* a piece of equipment, such as a toaster or stove, designed for a specific task
Mom got new appliances when she remodeled the kitchen.

applications: *n.* written requests
I had to fill out an application to work at the store.

approaching: *v.* moving close to; nearing
The car slowed down as the ducks began approaching the road.

automatically: *adv.* done right away without thought or control
The light by the garage went on automatically when we pulled in the driveway.

ballot: *n.* a piece of paper on which a voter marks a choice or choices
We selected class president by secret ballot.

benefits: *n.* things that improve life
The part-time job included a discount and many other benefits.

ceremony: *n.* a formal act in honor of an event or special occasion
I attended my cousin's wedding ceremony.

citizens: *n.* people who live in a country
The citizens of Canada elected a new leader.

colonies: *n.* the new place where groups of people settle
Someday we might start colonies on Mars.

command: *v.* to give orders to; direct
Our coach commanded us to run 10 laps.

competition: *n.* a contest
I competed in a state spelling competition.

connected: *v.* joined
The workman connected the satellite dish to our television.

conserve: *v.* to save or use carefully; to prevent waste
The teacher asked her students to conserve paper by writing on both sides.

contaminate: *v.* to make unclean or impure
Spilled chemicals contaminated the stream near my house.

continent: *n.* a giant piece of land on the earth
We live on the continent of North America.

data: *n.* information, facts and figures
We collected data before making the chart.

debris: *n.* scattered remains of something broken
After the storm, the road was covered with debris.

declared: *v.* to make known officially or with certainty
The mayor declared September 8th a town holiday.

deductions: *n.* the amount of money taken out of one's paycheck
I had a deduction from my paycheck for a vacation fund.

destructive: *adj.* harmful; causing damage
Our dog was very destructive when he was a puppy.

device: *n.* a piece of equipment
A pencil is a device for writing.

direction: *n.* path; course
The bus headed in the wrong direction.

displace: *v.* move out; force out
The floods displaced thousands of people from their houses.

distributed: *v.* handed out
The teacher distributed the new reading books.

donated: *v.* gave
Ivan donated his book collection to the library.

emit: *v.* to give off or send forth
The chocolate factory emits a strong odor into the air.

employees: *n.* workers
The grocery store hired many new employees.

environment: *n.* all of your surroundings
The child grew up in a loving environment.

eruption: *n.* explosion; sudden bursting forth
The volcano's eruption took everyone by surprise.

escapes: *v.* leaks out; gets free
Our hamster escapes from its cage about once a week.

exhausted: *adj.* very tired; worn out
Celina was exhausted after working all day in the garden.

experiments: *n.* tests done to find out something
We perform simple experiments in science class.

extreme: *adj.* great; strong
We had extreme cold this winter.

famine: *n.* a lack of food; a time of great hunger and starvation
When the crops failed, there was a famine.

fierce: *adj.* dangerous; powerful
The fierce winds blew down the power lines.

fuel: *n.* a substance that is burned to give off heat or energy
We searched for more fuel for the campfire.

gangplank: *n.* a board or ramp for people to walk from a ship to shore
The cruise passengers walked down the gangplank to reach the island.

illuminate: *v.* to shine light on
The street lights illuminated my neighbor's yard.

immigrants: *n.* people in a new country
The immigrants toured Washington, D.C.

income: *n.* the amount of money a person earns for a job
I put all of my babysitting income in the bank.

inland: *adv.* away from the coast
The weather is often warmer inland than at the beach.

international: *adj.* all over the world
The Internet makes international communication easy.

interview: *n.* meeting of people face to face
I had an interview with the manager for my new job.

launch: *v.* to send upward
The space shuttle will be launched next week.

located: *v.* found; placed
The police located the missing boy at the park.

loyal: *adj.* faithful in support of a person, country, or cause
The loyal employee worked at the company for 30 years.

majority: *n.* most
The majority of the class voted to delay the test.

material: *n.* substance from which something is made
Mom bought silk material to make a new dress.

opportunities: *n.* chances for things to happen
There are many opportunities to volunteer your time at school.

particles: *n.* tiny bits; specks
She wiped dust particles from the old book.

pollution: *n.* dirt and poisons in the air, ground, or water
Water pollution can kill many fish and plant life in rivers.

portion: *n.* a part of a whole
A portion of the lot will be used for a new playground.

pressure: *n.* force or strain of one thing against another
Tony felt the pressure of the heavy pack on his back.

pressure: *n.* a situation or event that causes concern
The pressure of having to do a report in front of the class made me nervous.

prevent: *v.* stop something before it happens
Brushing your teeth will help prevent cavities.

protect: *v.* to keep safe; guard
The robin sat on the nest to protect her eggs.

pursue: *v.* keep trying to achieve
My sister will pursue a career in law enforcement.

rapidly: *adv.* quickly
The storm passed through our town rapidly.

refineries: *n.* factories
The smoke from the sugar refinery filled the air with huge white clouds.

refund: *n.* an amount of money given back to a person
The salesperson gave John a refund when he returned the broken watch.

residents: *n.* people who live in a place
The residents of the apartment building were without power for three hours.

revenue: *n.* total amount of money collected
Julie used the revenue from her babysitting jobs to buy a stereo.

security: *n.* safety; something to help make things safe
A group of men and women provided security at the convention.

sensor: *n.* a device that detects and responds to a signal
The light went on when I passed by the sensor.

smog: *n.* a dirty layer of smoke and fog in the air
The smog above the big city hung in the air like a thick blanket.

site: *n.* the location of an event
Sydney, Australia was the site of the last Olympic Games.

sturdy: *adj.* strongly made or built
Dad helped build the sturdy tree fort.

survey: *v.* to look over or examine
The teacher surveyed the crowd for her class.

talent: *n.* a natural ability to do something well
José has a talent for playing the piano.

taxes: *n.* part of one's income paid to the government
The district raised taxes to build a new high school.

territory: *n.* area of land
Before Oregon became a state, it was called Oregon Territory.

tracking: *v.* following the course or path of something
The weatherman began tracking the snowstorm two days ago.

unattended: *adj.* not watched or cared for
The bank teller left the window unattended for several minutes.

unexpectedly: *adv.* without warning
It rained unexpectedly during the company picnic.

vacate: *v.* leave
The family vacated the apartment at the end of the month.

valuable: *adj.* of great importance
The goalie is a valuable member of a hockey team.

violent: *adj.* caused by great physical force
The dog's violent behavior scared many neighbors.

vote: *v.* to pick a candidate during an election
Sabrina will be able to vote in next year's election.

MY GLOSSARY
A–L

MY GLOSSARY
M–Z